Sacramento on the Air

SACRAMENTO on the Air

How the McClatchy Family Revolutionized West Coast Broadcasting

ANNETTE KASSIS

THE History PRESS

Published by The History Press
Charleston, SC
www.historypress.net

First published 2015

Manufactured in the United States

ISBN 978.1.62619.165.5

Library of Congress Control Number: 2015947034

For my grandmother Dovie Gilley Green.
I wish I had known you…I wonder what happened to you…
I hope someday we'll find you.
1895–?

CONTENTS

ACKNOWLEDGEMENTS

In the 1960s, when I was a child in Sacramento, my parents gave me a General Electric transistor radio. About three inches wide and less than five inches long, it came in a leatherette case with a strap that I found perfect for hanging on the handlebars of my bicycle. I kept the dial primarily set to Sacramento station KROY so I could listen to DJ "Wonder Rabbit," aka Martin Ashley.

Later, as a teenager living in northwest Louisiana, I spent many nights with my tabletop AM/FM radio carefully tuning the dial on the AM band to see what distant stations I might pick up. My favorite was WLS in Chicago, and I loved listening to John Records Landecker (Records truly is his middle name). I wrote to him when I was sixteen, and he sent me a T-shirt. At the time, I had no idea I was engaging in my own version of "distance listening." This practice of carefully tuning the radio receiver to pick up signals from distant stations was the primary activity of many radio enthusiasts in the 1920s, something I didn't know when I was trying to keep the volume low enough so my parents would not know I was still awake but loud enough to hear the broadcast.

As an adult, I've spent a significant part of my advertising career writing commercials for radio. I prefer to write for radio rather than television primarily because of radio's "theater of the mind" aspect—I can "show" anything on radio if I can get the listener to imagine it. Suffice it to say, radio is something in which I became interested at an early age, and I have never lost the fascination.

This book is a labor of love. It began its existence five years ago as my master's thesis—although this book is very different from my earlier academic work. I had thought it would be my first book; as it turns out, it's my third. But in revisiting the years of research I did for my thesis and in digging deeper into the lives of the people who make up this portion of Sacramento's broadcasting history, I realize those five years had to elapse between thesis and book before I could tell this story.

Between my thesis, which served as the starting point, and the completion of this work, there are many debts incurred and many people to thank.

California State University–Sacramento (CSUS) professors Chloe Burke and Scott Lupo formed my thesis committee and strongly supported my research interests. I'm pleased to say each has migrated from mentor to dear friend. I hope they are pleased to see the academic work rewritten as a more popular work.

My years as a "fixture" in the reading room at the Center for Sacramento History—the archive of the city and county of Sacramento, as well as the repository of some wonderful private collections—began when I was a graduate student. I am indebted to the help and support I've received through all my projects from city historian Marcia Eymann, deputy city historian Dylan McDonald, photographs archivist Rebecca Crowther and archivist Patricia Johnson.

Once again I tested friendship and family ties by relying on the talents of my two invaluable manuscript readers—Roma Heerhartz and Frances Rae. These two had to endure reading the early, clunky, problem-ridden draft of this work, and I thank them both for being so kind when they rendered their critique. This is the third time they have both served as readers and editors of my work in its early stages; either they are crazy, or they love me. I'd like to think they love me.

Roma, who has been reading my work for decades as my business partner in our advertising agency K&H Marketing, is so used to the idiosyncrasies in my early stage writing that I could practically pick out where I would find her notes in the early draft version of the manuscript. When she tells me a sentence is "awkward," I believe her.

When I discovered that my sister, Frances, was a top-notch editor in addition to being a wonderful sister, I immediately pressed her into service. That was three books ago. In addition to making wonderful suggestions about restructuring the manuscript for this book to its present form, she not only recommended the family tree and timeline but also researched all the family tree information for me. I owe her a great deal for that!

Acknowledgements

Writing might be done in solitude, but the writer relies heavily on family for support. My mother, Gertrude Loften Stout, who remains my biggest cheerleader, has never been one to lavish praise lightly, and so her words of encouragement mean the world to me. You are so right, mom, life is good.

Likewise my son, Michael Kassis, and my future daughter-in-law, Kayla Bettencourt, are solid in their support. Family means everything, and I am very proud of both of them. My husband, Rich Kassis, has endured the long weekends when I'm locked away writing, the evenings I'm not home because I'm researching and the inevitable pangs of doubt I feel in the early stages of working on a new book. Thanks to his solid support, I am able to keep going and push through the struggles that are always a part of this type of work.

Finally, I want to acknowledge a woman whom I have never met, but who is a very big part of me: my paternal grandmother, Dovie Gilley Green. Dovie suffered a great deal of loss and pain in her life—much of it from those who should have loved and protected her. Not knowing all the circumstances of her life and death has fueled my passion for digging into the stories of our American cultural past. Someday, I hope we will know what ultimately happened to her. When we do, I will surely write about it.

It is to her that I humbly dedicate this book.

McCLATCHY FAMILY TIMELINE AND LIST OF ACRONYMS

McCLATCHY FAMILY TIMELINE

James McClatchy and Charlotte Maria McCormack

James McClatchy

- Born in Ireland, 1824
- Arrived in New York circa 1844–46, having sailed from the port of Belfast
- Became naturalized citizen in New York on November 2, 1846
- Came to California circa 1849 (the gold rush)

Charlotte Maria McCormack

- Born in New Brunswick, Canada, of Irish-born parents
- Arrived in Sacramento from Canada circa 1852
- Was first married to Edward Feeney, 1853 (Feeney died in 1854)
- Married James McClatchy in 1856
- According to the 1900 census, she gave birth to nine children, four of whom survived:
    - Valentine Stuart McClatchy, born 1857
    - Charles Kenny (C.K.) McClatchy, born 1858
    - Mary F. (Fannie) McClatchy Richardson, born 1859
    - Emily Estelle McClatchy (never married), born 1860

Charles Kenny (C.K.) McClatchy and Elizabeth Ellen (Ella) Kelly

Charles Kenny (C.K.) McClatchy

- Born in Sacramento, California, on November 1, 1858

Elizabeth Ellen (Ella) Kelly

- Born in Philadelphia, Pennsylvania, on March 4, 1860
- Widowed mother brought the family to Sacramento by way of the Isthmus of Panama when Ella was a girl, sometime before 1870. The 1870 census shows the family in Sacramento with Ella, age ten.
- An interesting personal note about Ella McClatchy: many documents show her as born on March 4, 1861, and mention that it is the day of Abraham Lincoln's presidential inauguration. However, the 1860 census lists her at five months old. The fabrication about her being born on the day of Lincoln's inauguration persisted, presumably her intent, and is touted in various places and linked to the idea of her caring nature concerning the "poor and downtrodden."
- Married C.K. McClatchy in Sacramento on February 12, 1885 (Note: The tale about her birth on the day of Lincoln's inauguration dovetailed nicely with the fact that her wedding day was Abraham Lincoln's birthday.)
- Children:
    - Charlotte Estelle McClatchy, born on October 25, 1886 or 1887 (unclear)
    - Carlos Kelly McClatchy, born on March 2, 1891
    - Eleanor Grace McClatchy, born on September 27, 1896 (from passport application completed by Eleanor herself; some other records show her as born in 1895 or 1897)

Charlotte Estelle McClatchy and James Howard Maloney

Charlotte Estelle McClatchy

- Married James Howard Maloney in Spokane, Washington, on September 11, 1909
- Children
    - Martin J. Maloney, born on April 5, 1912
    - James Brown Maloney (called Brown Maloney), born on May 1, 1913

Carlos Kelly McClatchy and Phebe Briggs

Phebe Briggs

- Born on November 8, 1892
- Married Carlos Kelly McClatchy in Seattle, Washington, in January 1918
- Children
    - James Briggs McClatchy, born on December 17, 1920
    - William Ellery McClatchy, born on January 4, 1925
    - Charles Kenny McClatchy, born on March 25, 1927

Eleanor Grace McClatchy and Raymond L. Crozier

Eleanor Grace McClatchy

- Married Raymond L. Crozier in Sacramento circa 1920
- The marriage was annulled within a few years
- No children

LIST OF ACRONYMS

ABC American Broadcasting Company
AM Amplitude Modulation
ANPA American Newspaper Publishers Association
AP Associated Press
AT&T American Telephone & Telegraph
BBDO Batten, Barton, Durstine & Osborn Inc.
BCL Broadcast Listener
CBS Columbia Broadcasting System
CPM Cost Per Thousand
CRS California Radio System
FM Frequency Modulation
FRC Federal Radio Commission
FCC Federal Communications Commission
GE General Electric
INS International News Service
MBS Mutual Broadcasting System

NAB National Association of Broadcasters
NBC National Broadcasting Company
PNRC Publishers' National Radio Committee
PRB Press-Radio Bureau
UP United Press
RCA Radio Corporation of America

1

A BUZZ IN THE ETHER

Carlos is doing a good job. I cannot pay him a higher compliment than to say that he follows well in the footsteps of California's best editor.
—Hiram Johnson to C.K. McClatchy, 1920[1]

In 1921, Carlos McClatchy, the thirty-year-old son of Sacramento newspaper editor and publisher C.K. McClatchy and associate editor of the *Sacramento Bee*, visited a friend back East. The friend, who owned a radio receiver, passed the earphones to McClatchy and invited him to "listen to what's coming over the air." What McClatchy heard, possibly for the first time in his life, was the hiss, crackle, buzz and occasional music of the "ether"—the term for what "filled" the empty space around us. Excited by the new technology, he returned to Sacramento, where he convinced his father to invest company resources in Sacramento's first broadcast radio station. Wireless, as it was called at the time, was so new that many, including C.K. McClatchy, still regarded it as a toy, a hobby for young boys and dabbling amateurs. But Carlos was both enthusiastic and convincing, and the *Sacramento Bee* became the first newspaper on the Pacific coast—and one of the first newspapers in the country—to enter the business of radio broadcasting.[2]

Carlos McClatchy saw potential in wireless. As a newspaperman, he was in the business of reaching masses of people with information through the pages of the *Sacramento Bee*, and he recognized the possibility of reaching even more people with this new technology. His vision truly was on the forefront; at the time the *Sacramento Bee* went on the air in 1922 with its first broadcast radio station, KVQ, there were only seventy newspaper-owned radio stations in the United States out of 570 active radio stations across the country.[3] And most of those stations were located in the Midwest and Northeast, not out West.

The McClatchy Company and the McClatchy family entered broadcast radio at the industry's commercial beginnings with a single five-watt radio station that later grew, as KFBK, to a mere one hundred watts, where it stayed until 1935, well into radio's so-called golden age. When the McClatchys began their radio broadcasting enterprise, no one knew how to run the business of local radio, nor did they have any gauge of its potential. The *Sacramento Bee* approached its first radio station the same way it approached the newspapers: the media outlet serves a local audience, meets local needs and does not bow to outside influence.

James McClatchy, who came to California during the gold rush, was a founding editor of the *Daily Bee*. *Center for Sacramento History.*

Radio was different on the West Coast. In broadcasting's early decades, the Rocky Mountains formed a real "barrier" between the centers of network broadcasting in the East and the population of the western states. At the end of the 1930s, NBC may have had a broadcasting "lock" on two-thirds of the country's population by virtue of its affiliate stations, but those stations were predominantly located north of the Mason-Dixon line and stretched from New England to Omaha, Nebraska. The population of the West was considerably less dense than that of other parts of the country—why would early networks NBC or CBS put their primary focus on California? Why would anyone?

And yet California played a significant role in the development of broadcast radio as we know it. It cannot be overstated just how visionary it was for Carlos McClatchy to hear static in the ether and then translate his amazement into a business opportunity that brought broadcast radio to Sacramento in the form of the tiny, low-powered broadcast radio station KVQ.

And broadcast radio's beginnings did not so obviously point to the massive shift in communication that was to come.

BEFORE THE BUZZ

In 1912, an unsinkable ship hit an iceberg.

When the *Titanic* sank, it gave new urgency to the need to regulate the "ether." After the tragedy, reports circulated that a nearby ship had not responded to rescue calls because the wireless operator was off duty that night. In addition, newspapers reported that some amateur radio operators transmitted false reports that the *Titanic* had been safely towed to port. The horror at the loss of life and the seemingly careless or callous acts by radio amateurs led to action, and the loss of the *Titanic* spurred Congress to pass the Radio Act of 1912.[4]

For much of its early development, wireless, the precursor to broadcast radio, was unregulated in the United States. Although European nations agreed in 1903 and 1906 to establish international treaties regarding wireless communication, the United States did not follow suit. Wireless regulation was simply not a priority at a time when Congress was debating issues such as child labor and antitrust legislation.[5] But growing concerns over safety at sea in the wake of increasing interference from public and private wireless users eventually led Congress to approve the Radio Act of 1910.[6] The act mandated that any oceangoing vessel leaving a United States port and carrying fifty or more people must be outfitted with radio equipment, but the developing problem of interference from competing signals sent over the airwaves by military, commercial and amateur radio operators went unaddressed until the *Titanic* sank.[7]

In the wake of the *Titanic* tragedy, the Radio Act of 1912 brought new requirements for ships, and amateur operators were limited to the shortwave bands of the wireless spectrum.[8] Congress gave the secretary of commerce the power to assign wavelengths, but it did not give him the power to refuse to grant a license.[9] The presumption on the part of Congress was that the wireless spectrum was large enough to accommodate all who wanted a license to operate a radio station.[10]

Radio broadcasting was like the Wild West.

REGULATING THE ETHER

In this decade prior to KVQ's initial broadcast, wireless had been a wide-open landscape sparsely populated by amateurs who built their

Above and opposite: Elizabeth Ellen (Ella) Kelly and Charles Kenny (C.K.) McClatchy married in Sacramento in 1885. *Center for Sacramento History*.

own equipment to receive and, in some cases, transmit the signals. By 1912, wireless telegraphy (the wireless sending of dots and dashes) gave way to radiotelephony (the transmission of the human voice). The number of amateurs dabbling in wireless grew significantly after 1912, when the Department of Commerce published a "call book" naming all amateurs who had passed the government-licensing test. Now these amateurs had a sense of just how many others like themselves were scattered across the country sending, receiving and listening.[11] But in 1917, when the United States declared war on Germany, all amateurs were ordered to close and dismantle their stations. In some cases, German Americans who had wireless stations were questioned on charges of espionage, their stations were destroyed and their homes were ransacked.[12]

Wireless was important to the war effort, however, and many of the amateurs put their skills to use for the military during World War I. In 1919, the federal government lifted the ban on both amateur receiving and amateur transmitting, but all those licenses suspended when the United States entered the war had to be reissued. By the fall of 1919, the amateurs were transmitting again.[13] When the U.S. government took control of all those wireless stations during the war, it also issued guarantees to competing manufacturers, assuring them they would be protected from any patent infringement lawsuits.[14] The goal was to create an atmosphere conducive to innovative research and production and to protect wireless use for military purposes during wartime.[15]

Wartime technical development and the interest it created propelled the fledgling broadcast industry forward, and amateurs were eager to get their hands on the new technology.

After the war, in an effort to promote U.S. influence in international communications, which at the time was dominated by Great Britain via British Marconi, the federal government facilitated a series of negotiations that ultimately resulted in the creation of the Radio Corporation of America (RCA). This effort of private enterprise and government brought together General Electric (GE) and its new acquisitions American Marconi, American Telephone & Telegraph (AT&T) and AT&T's subsidiary Western Electric.[16] The creation of RCA allowed the companies involved to pool their patents and divide the business. GE manufactured receivers and parts to be marketed through RCA, and AT&T sold the transmitters and controlled all aspects of telephony service, whether by wire or wireless.[17] The companies involved in RCA controlled multiple aspects of radio technology, giving them a tremendous advantage in the growing industry. Broadcasting, however, was not the goal. Point-to-point communication, such as existed with the telephone, was the perceived area in which these companies thought profitable business development lay.[18]

At the time, the radio industry did not know how "broadcasting" could possibly make money. Who would be listening? More to the point, what could a broadcast radio listener possibly hope to hear?

Above: Ella (center) with her children Charlotte Estelle McClatchy and Carlos Kelly McClatchy. *Opposite*: The McClatchy children: Charlotte, Carlos and Eleanor Grace McClatchy. *Center for Sacramento History*.

IS THERE ANYBODY OUT THERE?

RCA began selling new wartime-developed tubes capable of transmitting speech and music to the general public in the spring of 1921. The subsequent rise in amateur use revealed an intense interest in what might be "out there" to which these enthusiasts could listen.[19] This is the point at which Carlos McClatchy would have first listened to the radio receiver at his friend's home and formulated the idea that the *Sacramento Bee* should embrace the new technology.

For many of radio's early listeners, the owner of the station and the content of the broadcast were far less important than the station's call signal. "Distance listening" was the primary focus of many early radio enthusiasts, with radio magazines arranging contests for the most miles logged through tuning the receiver to pick up a distant station. Indeed, for these early listeners, those who had built their own receivers and spent their evenings "fishing" for far-off signals, station identification was the main item for which they listened.[20] As the number of broadcast stations grew, interest in listening grew as well. This trend created a conflict between the engineering and technical-focused amateurs and the general "broadcast listener," or BCL. BCLs did not bother to learn anything about the technology itself or the proper methods of tuning a receiver, creating problems for neighbors with their own receivers. On the other side of the argument, the BCLs blamed the amateurs for all manner of signal interference, which impacted the BCLs' primary goal of listening to broadcast content. Amateurs saw broadcasting as just one application of the technology; these amateurs also wanted to communicate with one another, receive news and agricultural reports and actively participate in development and advancements in the technology.[21]

The amateurs did not define broadcasting as large stations sending programs over the air to a mass audience of BCLs who had no clue how the program got there or, worse, did not care.

In addition to the differing points of view of the amateurs and the BCLs, there were also conflicting opinions about how radio should be used. Some saw radio as a means of education, "moral uplift" and a tool to combat the "debasing effects of mass culture," as well as a means of assimilating "millions of foreigners."[22] A 1923 article in *Radio Broadcast* boldly asserted that radio must be used to conquer an "insidious" enemy, the unassimilated foreigner (the term "immigrant" is not used by the article's author). "Each is a parasite living upon the natural resources and under the protection offered by America, yet giving little or nothing in return."[23] This group, the author stated, included not just recent immigrants, but those millions who enjoyed American citizenship and all its privileges but who secretly clung to the ways of their native country. Radio, the writer posed, would not only teach a familiarity with American political and social ideals but would also instruct the newcomer in "correct English." "English correctly heard is English correctly spoken, and the foreigner landing on a strange shore is almost as imitative as a child."[24]

It was not just immigrants whom social critics and reformers felt would benefit from a healthy dose of culture over the airwaves. Some felt radio

As a newspaper family, the McClatchys had influence. This photograph shows Eleanor, C.K. and Ella in front of their home with three-time presidential candidate and U.S. secretary of state William Jennings Bryan (second from right), circa 1919. *Center for Sacramento History.*

should be the tool by which people in rural areas were put on more of a cultural par with urbanites in terms of their access to information and their exposure to elements of higher culture, such as classical music. But an unintended consequence was that radio also became the means by which people in rural areas adopted more of the consumerism traits of urban residents.[25]

While radio was lauded as a means of cultural uplift, it was also vilified as the medium became advertiser-supported and commercial interests assumed the lead in developing broadcasting. An editorial in a 1924 issue of the *New Republic* strongly criticized that radio "is mainly under control of men unfitted by training and personality for posts of such importance." Businessmen, it continued, could not understand the "proper use" of the medium and were indifferent to that proper use anyway. But as one historian noted, if radio was corporate controlled, it had to turn a profit. And the way had been paved for corporate control almost since the beginning when, in 1912, preferred assignments on the wireless spectrum were given to commercial wireless companies and the military while other users were assigned the less desirable wavelengths. In the 1920s, Secretary of Commerce Herbert Hoover dealt with the "chaos of the ether" by creating three classes of broadcast radio stations: high, medium and low. High-powered stations got the most desirable and least congested wavelengths. Not coincidentally, radio stations owned by AT&T, General Electric and Westinghouse were high powered, and the stations of universities, churches and labor unions were low powered.[26]

To put this in perspective, KVQ, the *Sacramento Bee* station jointly owned with local entrepreneur J.C. Hobrecht, was assigned a wavelength in the low-power category at 360 meters and allowed to broadcast on a limited schedule and at only five watts initially.

But even at just five watts, Sacramento had its own radio station when many other places in the United States did not.

WHO WAS REALLY FIRST?

The new medium of broadcast radio took a leap forward just after World War I at a time when consumer spending rose and postwar prosperity provided a new mass market for advertisers. The American consumer society flourished as wages increased, more women began working for wages, population growth in urban areas outpaced population numbers in rural areas and many of the basic necessities were no longer made at home but purchased at department stores. Newly affluent Americans sought brand-name products and the status and identity that came with them.[27] This was a time of rapid cultural and social change as America moved from being a predominantly rural society to a mostly urban one with a growing taste for consumer goods.[28]

By the early 1920s, when Carlos McClatchy was working with his father, the *Bee* was the dominant Sacramento daily newspaper, surpassing one rival morning paper, the *Sacramento Union*, and acquiring another, the Scripps-owned *Sacramento Star*.[29] As a well-established, powerful and growing newspaper well versed in the business of media as it existed in the early 1920s, the *Sacramento Bee*, in hindsight, was perfectly poised to enter the new medium of broadcast radio. But in 1922, when Sacramento's first radio station went on the air, broadcast radio was a largely untested medium from a business standpoint. Radio had undetermined potential, an undeveloped audience and unknown costs of operation.

Other companies were also eyeing the fledgling technology, among them Westinghouse Electric and Manufacturing Company. Westinghouse came at the radio industry from a different direction. Frank Conrad, a Westinghouse employee, had been using his own transmitter to air a music program from his home in Pittsburgh, Pennsylvania. As a hobbyist, Conrad was interested in giving other amateur radio enthusiasts, or "hams," something to hear when they tuned in. Westinghouse executives noticed an upsurge in the sales of radio receiving equipment when these broadcasts aired and, sensing an opportunity, moved Conrad's transmitter to the roof of the Westinghouse building, applied for a federal license and began broadcasting as KDKA in 1920.[30] Credited by many historians with broadcasting the first radio program, KDKA's transmission of the Harding-Cox presidential election returns was heard on fewer than one thousand receivers.[31]

Not all historians agree with KDKA's claim of being first, however. It is understandable that the KDKA story would have gained such traction—the station was owned by a company that was key in radio's development after all, and KDKA is located near the center of industry and regulatory power for the fledgling industry. But that honor, some believe, rightly belongs to a San Jose, California amateur named Charles Herrold and his wife, Sybil Paull Herrold True.

Charles "Doc" Herrold was regularly broadcasting music and advertising to a local California audience as early as 1914,[32] perhaps even earlier.

THE FIRST COUPLE OF BROADCAST RADIO

The question of "who was first" has been debated by those involved in the development of broadcast radio, amateur broadcasters, commercial broadcast radio stations and historians. A lot depends on your selection of terms and how you define what, exactly, is a radio broadcast.

Canadian-born inventor Reginald Fessenden, who at a young age worked with Thomas Edison from 1887 to 1890, claimed responsibility for the oldest broadcast—a Christmas Eve program aired in 1906.[33]

Fessenden defined broadcasting as the transmission of speech, music and singing to receiving stations operated by firms other than the sending station. He also pointed out that for true broadcasting to take place, such a program would also have to be advertised, giving potential listeners advance notice that a program would air. Fessenden's Christmas Eve program began with a short speech by the inventor telling listeners what to expect. He played phonograph records, performed "O, Holy Night" as a violin solo, sang one verse of "Adore and Be Still," read "Glory to God in the highest and on earth peace to men of good will" from the Bible and ended by wishing everyone a Merry Christmas and announcing that the program would be repeated on New Year's Eve. The Christmas Eve broadcast had been advertised three days in advance by telegraph—ships belonging to the U.S. Navy and the United Fruit Company and equipped with Fessenden's receiving apparatus were notified of the impending broadcast.[34]

Fessenden's work might have been the first broadcast, but unlike Doc and Sybil, he did not continue the practice on a regular time schedule.

"THIS IS CHARLES D. HERROLD'S SCHOOL OF WIRELESS IN SAN JOSE"

Charles D. Herrold, affectionately called "Doc" or "Prof" by his students, opened his school of radio on January 1, 1909, in San Jose, and from the beginning, daily broadcasts were part of the routine.

By early 1912, Herrold had installed a receiving set in a local music store with twenty-four telephone receivers so customers could listen to the music being broadcast. Shortly thereafter, when Doc met and married the much younger Sybil Paull in 1913, she got into broadcasting as well. If Doc can be credited with the first radio broadcasting station, then Sybil can be credited with being the first woman disc jockey and running the first on-air radio promotion. By 1914 or 1915, Sybil had her own program. She and Doc made arrangements with a San Jose music store so they would have an unlimited supply of records to play. Sybil borrowed the records from the Sherman and Clay store, and in return, she would advertise the records. "We would play all the up-to-date young people's records," she recalled in an interview, "and they would be sure to run down the next day to buy the one they heard on the radio the night before."[35]

Sybil would announce that this was "KQW calling and that this was their Wednesday night program." As part of the program, which aired each Wednesday at 8:00 p.m., Sybil asked "the little hams," as she called the young listeners, to come in to the record store and sign their name, where they lived and where they had their receiving set. KQW gave away a prize each week, like a new galena (crystal radio) set or a pair of headphones. "Well these little boys would come from all over the valley here and come in and register and get acquainted," Sybil said. "And in that way we became acquainted with all the boys who were interested." This was 1914 or 1915.[36]

Doc began by broadcasting with a spark transmitter and then with an arc transmitter. Getting the power to operate the arc transmitter is a story to rival any in the early days of broadcasting. As one of the "little hams" who later worked with Doc—Joseph D. Cappa—recalled, Doc and his students were hijacking power from the streetcar lines:

> *Well, we had a long bamboo pole with a hook on it that we used to hook over the trolley wire and then pull it up from the roof...Later on, the streetcar company couldn't figure out why they ran one streetcar a night down South First Street and they used up 9 kw of energy for a couple of hours in a row. So they found that this was being tapped. They came in and told* [Doc] *that rather than see him risking the kids' lives every night that they'd put a meter in and give him the power.*[37]

Although Doc Herrold had been assigned the call letters KQW, he usually did not announce them. As one listener remembered, when Doc was on the air he would say, "This is Charles D. Herrold's school of wireless in San Jose," rather than, "This is KQW." KQW, operating continually since Doc's 1909 start—with the exception of the enforced broadcast hiatus of World War I—became KCBS in San Francisco in 1949 and is still on the air.

So why does the argument persist? Doc and Sybil Herrold and their students were clearly broadcasting entertainment programming, advertising and contests years before KDKA staked its claim as the first. Many people were—and still are—irked by KDKA's claim, including former "little ham" Joseph Cappa:

> *I talked to Prof several times in Oakland and asked him why he let KDKA get away with their claim. Prof told me that KDKA made the claim that they were the first licensed* commercial station *on the air. He was not a commercial station; he was an experimental. Prof was the first broadcaster, and he was such a swell fellow that it just irritated me to see that a man of his ability and character did not get the credit that was due to him. I think he was the first broadcaster and I think that he should be given that credit. He certainly deserves it.*[38]

2
"SACRAMENTO BEE CALLING, HELLO, HELLO"

I have no radio, for which I sometimes thank God.
—C.K. McClatchy, 1928

In 1920, the general radio audience consisted of thousands of amateur set builders, most interested simply in logging distances listened. In New York in 1922, an experimental station operated by AT&T—WEAF—aired what, in spite of "Doc" Herrold's much earlier work, has been deemed the first commercial—a five minute real estate advertisement for an apartment building named Hawthorne Court. A number of apartment units were sold simply on the strength of the broadcast.[39] Within a year, WEAF had twenty-five sponsors, including Macy's, Colgate and Metropolitan Life Insurance. The station soon changed its call letters to WNBC when RCA purchased the station from AT&T.[40] Increasingly, there was something "out there" for a general audience of listeners as the number of licensed radio stations leapt from a mere thirty at the end of 1920, to 576 in early 1923.[41] One of these new stations was Sacramento's first—KVQ, licensed to electrical appliance store owner J.C. Hobrecht on December 9, 1921.[42]

The new station went on the air two months later.

At some point between the issuance of the license and the inaugural broadcast of KVQ, Hobrecht and Carlos McClatchy struck the business arrangement that moved the fledgling station's broadcast equipment to the top of the *Sacramento Bee* building on Seventh Street between I and J Streets and solidified the *Bee*'s pioneering role in West Coast broadcasting.[43]

Amateur radio enthusiast and electrical appliance store owner J.C. Hobrecht obtained the initial license for KVQ before partnering with Carlos McClatchy. *Center for Sacramento History*.

An amateur radio enthusiast himself, Hobrecht's store began selling wireless components in 1913. His primary customers for these materials were local schoolboys—not unlike Sybil Herrold's "little hams"—who were able to assemble working transmitters and receivers from the cheap, simple parts Hobrecht carried.[44] For J.C. Hobrecht, radio held possibilities that would enhance his electrical business. Hobrecht, who had already made a name for himself locally as the designer and patent holder of sections of Sacramento's recently installed street lighting system, now saw an opportunity to sell more components by giving local radio amateurs something to listen to, something for which it would be worth building a receiver.[45]

J.C. HOBRECHT, CARLOS McCLATCHY AND SACRAMENTO'S FIRST RADIO STATION

The station went on the air at 5:30 p.m. on February 2, 1922, with the words, "KVQ, KVQ, KVQ—*Sacramento Bee* calling. Hello. Hello." Listeners heard musical numbers by the Victor Eight, "all stars of the Victor Record Company," in town for a performance later that evening at the Clunie Theater. The inaugural broadcast concluded at 6:30 p.m., a mere one hour later, in keeping with the regulations of KVQ's license. The following day, the *Bee* carried detailed directions for making a wireless set. Promising the reader, "Study these directions and you will be able to construct an inexpensive receiving apparatus and hear the Bee's concerts and news service," there is little doubt the required materials were readily available from J.C. Hobrecht's store.[46]

For the remainder of 1922, the *Bee* promoted KVQ in articles that described the role the station played in the community and how far the

The *Sacramento Bee* building on Seventh Street also housed KVQ. *Center for Sacramento History*.

The Eight Famous Victor Artists, or the Victor Eight, were the first performers broadcast on KVQ. *Photograph by Rebecca Crowther.*

KVQ broadcasts carried. But interest in the station could neither be developed nor sustained, at least not to the level expected. By December, the station was closed.[47]

But the brief initial existence of KVQ was enough to solidify the *Sacramento Bee*'s position in West Coast broadcasting history as, reportedly, the first newspaper on the Pacific coast to operate a radio station. On the surface, this seems an unlikely scenario. *Bee* editor C.K. McClatchy showed no interest in or understanding of the new medium of radio. As late as 1928, he wrote to his friend Senator Hiram Johnson and claimed, "I have no radio, for which I sometimes thank God."[48]

It was Carlos who continued to pursue radio and eventually established a multi-station broadcasting company after KVQ's demise. For Carlos, radio broadcasting was not a threat to the "Fourth Estate," as other journalists and publishers came to regard it; Carlos saw radio as an additional means of public service.[49]

This is the key to the mindset of Carlos McClatchy that allowed the McClatchy Company to take a lead in newspaper-owned broadcast radio.

From KVQ to KFBK

In 1922, the year the *Bee* and Hobrecht went on the air as KVQ, newspapers and other publications were not the primary owners of broadcasting stations. Carlos McClatchy's vision put the *Bee* years ahead of competitors like William Randolph Hearst. It would be another six years before Hearst would be able to convince his newspaper publishers on the West Coast to buy local radio stations and actively use them to promote the Hearst publications.[50] At this time, radio and "electric" manufacturers and dealers made up approximately 41 percent of businesses engaged in broadcasting. As in the case of Westinghouse and Frank Conrad, these businesses saw broadcasting as a means to sell the components required for radio listening—there was considerably less concern over broadcasting as an end to itself. The remaining broadcast radio station owners ran an interesting gamut. Nationally, publications composed about 12 percent of station ownership. Fifteen percent of the station owners were classified as "unknown" occupation, 11 percent were educational institutions and 21 percent came from a variety of industries and organizations, including churches, banks, auto dealers, department stores, railroads and hardware stores, as well as one radio station owned by a laundry.[51]

Many of these small, low-powered community stations disappeared when the expense of operating the station exceeded the perceived benefit derived from listener "good will" or when the federal regulations enacted after 1927 took effect.

By 1924, some newspapers had already given up their broadcasting experiments. Others, however, maintained their radio stations as a means of generating that important "good will" for the newspapers. Those newspaper owners no longer on the air maintained that the expense of broadcasting and station maintenance was not worth the money. The newspapers that continued to operate broadcast radio stations, however, felt they would "reap our reward in good will, by helping directly and indirectly to serve the public."[52] A radio enthusiast interviewed for a story in *Radio Broadcast* magazine in 1924 was asked if he thought radio broadcasting helped a newspaper. "I don't see how radio can avoid doing that very thing," he responded. "Where I formerly bought one paper, I now buy two and sometimes three, for I don't want to miss any of the programs, near or far!"[53] There was value in a newspaper maintaining a viable public presence, especially in the face of head-to-head competition with one or more daily newspapers in the same city.[54] This form of public service, it was hoped, would enhance circulation as well as public image.

The *Sacramento Bee*'s initial foray into broadcasting might have ended with the demise of KVQ in December 1922, but Carlos McClatchy's interest in broadcasting continued and escalated. By 1925, the *Bee* had returned to broadcasting with KFBK, a station originated by the Kimball-Upson Company in 1922 shortly after KVQ went on the air.

And one of the new components of McClatchy-operated KFBK was an overt interest in on-air advertising.

On September 1, 1925, the James McClatchy Company entered into an agreement with Kimball-Upson to jointly operate KFBK, referred to contractually as "The *Bee*—Kimball-Upson Station." It is unclear who contacted whom first or if the negotiations were conducted by or at the behest of Carlos McClatchy, but under the terms of the agreement the McClatchy Company would pay all operation and maintenance expenses for the station and assume the cost of enlarging the studio. For half interest in the KFBK license, equipment and good will, McClatchy placed a $3,000 credit on its books for Kimball-Upson to use for its store advertising in the *Sacramento Bee*, under the rate and terms of a standard twelve-month contract. In return, the McClatchy Company retained the right to sell advertising on KFBK at

The Kimball-Upson Company, selling sporting goods, Majestic Radios and other items, partnered with the *Sacramento Bee* in the license for KFBK. *Center for Sacramento History*.

whatever rate McClatchy desired. Any net profit from the advertising venture was to be divided equally between the two partners up to $6,000. McClatchy would then retain 80 percent of the advertising net profit above $6,000.[55]

KFBK was not the only radio station owned by the McClatchy Company in 1925. Carlos, now editor of the *Fresno Bee* since it began in 1922, had also negotiated to buy Fresno station KMJ.[56] Both stations actively sold broadcast advertising.

SELLING ADVERTISING AND BUILDING AN AUDIENCE

Some historians stand firmly by the assertion that Americans did not desire advertising over the radio. Secretary of Commerce Herbert Hoover himself supposedly argued against the practice. Advertising on the radio existed almost since the beginning, however—all the way back to "Doc" and Sybil Herrold's experimental broadcast radio station in San Jose. But much of the history of American radio, including the history of radio advertising, has focused on the development of the networks and especially large radio stations in the Northeast and the Midwest, their programming and their policies.

Radio was different for stations like KFBK, KMJ and other small, local stations, however. Such independent stations have been regarded in a number of histories of radio broadcasting as locally oriented and somewhat "low-brow" from a cultural perspective.[57] But while Hoover's keynote address at the First National Radio Conference might have declared it "inconceivable that we should allow so great a possibility for service to be drowned in advertising chatter," the Commerce Department did not *forbid* advertising on the radio, and most Americans simply did not object to it.[58] Hoover's inconsistencies toward broadcasting are not surprising given that, as secretary of commerce, he also spoke against monopolies and vested interests, as well as excessive advertising, yet continued to acquiesce to dominant business groups in areas of commerce policy.[59]

The McClatchy Company was most certainly interested in selling advertising on air, as evidenced not only by their ownership agreement with Kimball-Upson but also by their business correspondence as well. As a rule, newspapers that owned radio stations viewed the station not as a separate income-generating business but as a means of promoting the newspaper. At the time, a newspaper had very little means of advertising itself. Without radio, billboards were about the only alternative medium for newspaper promotion. The radio editor of the *Chicago Daily News*, William S. Hedges, regarded newspaper ownership of radio as important not because the station could be an additional source of revenue but because of the good will for the newspaper. "The creation of good will, that intangible, yet nevertheless invaluable asset for quasi-public institutions, such as newspapers, results from our broadcasting. Dollars may not directly follow from the pleasures experienced by listeners…but the feeling of friendliness is there, and the friendship of the masses makes strength for the newspaper."[60]

While Carlos McClatchy understood the importance of good will for the newspapers, he was also a businessman who knew an opportunity when he saw one.

Once the agreement with Kimball-Upson was signed in 1925, the McClatchy Company began immediate investigation into selling advertising on KFBK. Since other newspaper publishing companies that owned radio stations were considering the same course of action, W.H. James, the *Bee*'s business director, sought the advice of the American Newspaper Publishers Association (ANPA) regarding rules and regulations governing the sale of time on the air.[61] As the Bee began putting together its rate card for broadcast advertising sales, it was looking at KFBK in much the same way it regarded the newspaper in terms of using circulation as a determinant of advertising rates. In a memo to Carlos McClatchy about the rate card just received from the *Oregonian*, W.H. James wrote, "I am astonished to note that they are selling time for courtesy concerts at $15 for day hours and from $25 to $40 an hour for evening hours. This, however, does not, I think, need to bother us particularly because I imagine that even though they have a much more powerful station, their available listeners-in for advertisers are far fewer in numbers than we will have under the guns of our station."[62] James anticipated Sacramento's potential audience for station broadcasts would be larger than that of Portland, Oregon, and the *Sacramento Bee* intended to charge advertisers accordingly.

Choosing to sell advertising, however, was a far different prospect than *actually* selling it. In an era when advertising agencies still did not know how to effectively write for the medium of radio, salesmen most certainly did not know how to sell for it. For the *Sacramento Bee*, building a sales department for KFBK took a concerted effort and considerable resources. Station KFI in Los Angeles had been over this ground already and advised its northern California broadcast neighbor to find someone with general sales experience and then educate him or her about radio. "We have gone through more or less grief in building [the advertising] department…It seems that the average newspaper solicitor just doesn't seem to fit."[63]

Advertising sold on McClatchy stations at this time was indirect; a sponsor's name was allowed but no "sales pitch." Airtime sold for "advertising or sales talks of any kind" was strictly forbidden until competition eventually forced management's hand.[64] In 1928, KFBK program director R.K. Clark, writing to W.H. James, referenced the possibility of a competing station attempting to come into the Sacramento market. He suggested a preemptive plan of attack that included moving the transmitter and studios to a location more suitable for broadcasting; making a "reasonable reduction" in advertising rates to $65, $50 and $40 per hour depending on the time of day aired; and changing the present policy regarding direct advertising. Noting that many of the "old conservative broadcasters"—KFI in Los Angeles, KFRC in San Francisco and KGO in Oakland—had begun accepting direct advertising, there would be "no lost dignity for KFBK if we accept this type of advertising, when every other station in the country is doing it."[65]

A follow-up memo from Clark outlined the source of the potential competition. George Turner, owner of KWG in Stockton, had been to Sacramento recently, scouting locations for a remote control studio—a studio that would have been operated by means of telephone lines to broadcast points distant to the transmitting station. Clark reported that Turner had approached a number of Sacramento advertisers and attempted to hire away KFBK's station operator. In a move that was, on the one hand, arrogantly self-confident and, on the other, an admission of the importance of newspaper promotion for radio stations, Turner approached Clark and asked that KWG's programs be listed in the *Sacramento Bee*. The request was politely but firmly denied.[66]

Sacramento would remain a city with only one radio station until 1937.

3

JUST WHO IS "THE PUBLIC?"

The officers of Kimball-Upson Company this morning discussed the matter of the Broadcast Station along the lines of our conversation. The general sentiment was that we look with favor upon getting out of the Station.
—A.I. Maginnis, 1928

In 1928, the reception area at KFBK featured a large map of the Western Hemisphere across one wall. Listeners from around the country wrote to the station, and when a letter from a new locale was received, a pin went into the map to mark the spot. The map had pins in every state. There were even pins representing a listener on board a ship three hundred miles off the Atlantic coast and a fan in Kentville, Nova Scotia, Canada.[67] The *Sacramento Bee*'s low-powered radio broadcast signal was certainly making its way around.

Broadcast businesses like KFBK were moving forward; however, the path was anything but certain.

Both the developing McClatchy media holdings in particular and broadcast radio in general experienced a fair amount of upheaval as the still young industry of radio broadcasting encountered legislative opposition. For the McClatchy Company, the assault by KWG came close on the heels of a fight to control signal interference, unexpected signal reallocation and new limits placed on the broadcast day. As the federal government began to more heavily regulate broadcasting, KFBK had to defend itself and its existence using a new and poorly defined standard—the public interest.

"CLEAR CHANNEL," "PROPAGANDA" AND AN EVANGELIST IN THE CROSSHAIRS

McClatchy's concerns over impending broadcast regulations arose during the Sixty-Ninth Congress as the House and Senate each passed bills intent on tighter regulation of radio broadcasting.[68]

The McClatchys followed the proceedings closely through family friend Senator Hiram Johnson. One of the provisions of the legislation was the intent to uphold all United States laws relating to "unlawful restraints and monopolies."[69] This section of the proposed Radio Act, along with the sections against monopolies and ownership of a combination of radio and wire systems, were directed at RCA and AT&T, which independent broadcasters and some members of Congress considered a joint monopoly. Combined, RCA and AT&T held radio equipment patents, transmission lines and ownership of eleven radio stations, including the four largest in the country, WGY, KDKA, WJZ and WEAF, which represented almost one-third of the broadcasting power allotted to all radio stations in the United States.[70]

The compromise bill between the House and Senate—the White-Dill Radio Bill—included a vague "public interest, convenience and necessity" standard to be used in granting and renewing licenses for broadcasters, created a five-member Federal Radio Commission (FRC) and divided the country into five broadcast zones: zone one, Maine, New Hampshire, Vermont, Massachusetts, Connecticut, Rhode Island, New York, New Jersey, Delaware, Maryland, the District of Columbia, Puerto Rico and the Virgin Islands; zone two, Pennsylvania, Virginia, West Virginia, Ohio, Michigan and Kentucky; zone three, North and South Carolina, Georgia, Florida, Alabama, Tennessee, Mississippi, Arkansas, Louisiana, Texas and Oklahoma; zone 4, Indiana, Illinois, Wisconsin, Minnesota, North and South Dakota, Iowa, Nebraska, Kansas and Missouri; and zone five, Montana, Idaho, Wyoming, Colorado, New Mexico, Arizona, Utah, Nevada, Washington, Oregon, California, the Territory of Hawaii and Alaska.[71] On February 23, Congress passed the compromise bill, the Radio Act of 1927.

By June, the FRC had begun making new assignments of wavelengths in accordance with its interpretation of the Radio Act and the new public interest standard. For broadcast station owners like the McClatchys, that meant a forced scramble of stations up and down the dial.

All broadcasters had to reapply for their licenses following passage of the Radio Act of 1927, and the bias shown toward large commercial stations was very clear. In the signal reallocation by the FRC, of the twenty-four "clear channel signals"—those signals not shared with other stations—twenty-one were awarded to network affiliates of NBC or CBS. "Propaganda" stations, such as the many stations operated by religious groups, universities and small local broadcasters like the McClatchys, had to share frequencies.[72] When stations shared frequencies, their amount of broadcast time was limited. A 1928 broadcast schedule for KFBK published in the *Sacramento Bee*, for example, shows broadcast hours limited to between 7:30 p.m. and 10:00 p.m.

Many broadcasters were business owners who had already poured considerable resources into the development of their broadcast radio operations. Now they were required to adhere to a new standard, one that applied to both programming content and technical matters, such as frequency allocation and signal strength. In determining who should be licensed, the FRC based its decision not only on which applicants could provide what the FRC considered general programming in the public interest—classical and light music, entertainment, information, weather and other offerings of a general appeal—but which licensees had the technical means to provide the best service. This, of course, favored those broadcasters with financial means over poorly financed, small broadcasters. It also made the FRC the arbiter of what the American public should hear.

KFBK's one-hundred-watt station was reassigned to a frequency of 560 kilocycles, resulting in some interference from KMTR in Hollywood, assigned to a frequency of 570 kilocycles and broadcasting with five hundred watts of power. KFBK tolerated the initial change—after all, what choice did the McClatchy Company really have—but when the Kimball-Upson and McClatchy companies received word that KGA in Spokane, Washington, had applied to the FRC for a power increase to twenty thousand watts and a frequency of 550 kilocycles, KFBK protested to the FRC and used the public interest standard to do it. Saying that KFBK was built for the "sole purpose of serving the Sacramento Valley" and that it provided a "high type" of broadcast entertainment and educational programming, station partner Kimball-Upson Company noted KFBK's "continuous operation under rigid regulations since the latter part of 1922" and that "this station has come to be recognized as one of the pioneer radio stations not only in the West, but of the country." Specifying that KFBK's operators have always taken a public service approach and not a mercenary one, the Kimball-Upson letter pointed out that the station always cooperated fully with regulations and suggestions of the FRC and always respected the broadcast rights of others. Interference from a high-powered station to the north would "practically obliterate the effectiveness of this station and destroy the clientele which it has built up during…continuous operation."[73]

The point was moot.

The KGA reassignment to 550 kilocycles did not occur, nor did KFBK remain at 560 kilocycles. The FRC determined that the public interest would best be served by moving KFBK to 1,090 kilocycles, a frequency it would share with KTBI in Los Angeles, keeping KFBK at a low 100 watts of power and limiting the Sacramento station's broadcast schedule to Tuesday, Wednesday, Thursday and Saturday from 6:00 p.m. to 10:00 p.m.[74] W.H. James of the McClatchy Company wasted no time in responding to the situation. His major concern was the frequency allocation; 1,090 kilocycles was a mere 10 kilocycles away from newly reassigned KEX of Portland, Oregon, broadcasting with 2,500 watts of power.[75] Before this situation could be settled, however, the parameters for allocating broadcast frequencies changed yet again.

The nationwide signal reallocation and the ensuing complaints of broadcasters across the country reflected both disagreement with the FRC's initial interpretation of the Radio Act of 1927 and the general lack of technical knowledge in Congress about radio broadcasting and how broadcast signals travel. Frustrated over perceived inequities of frequency distribution, House and Senate members from the four FRC zones outside New York–dominated zone one pushed through the Davis Amendment to the Radio Act of 1927.[76]

Named for Tennessee representative E.L. Davis, the amendment required the FRC to distribute wavelengths and broadcasting power equally among the five FRC zones based on population, ignoring geographical considerations such as terrain, physical distance from the signal transmission and circular reach of a broadcast signal.[77] The intent was to make the distribution of frequencies, hours of broadcast and station power equitable among the five zones with particular attention paid to the southern states in which existing broadcast radio stations were lacking.

But the result was that Pacific region zone five stations like KFBK faced difficulty acquiring more power and staving off encroaching interference from stronger stations.

For these political reasons, Carlos McClatchy's attempt to bring KFBK up to one thousand watts of power was contingent upon a successful petition to take the frequency and power of another California station, thereby maintaining the "equitable" balance in zone five. "All the commissioners agreed that the two [California] valleys were entitled to thousand watt stations," Carlos wrote to W.H. James, "but as California is overpowered now and the other districts underpowered, naturally the commissioners from the other districts refused to penalize their own areas by granting California more." If the wattage were taken from other California stations, Carlos continued, the FRC would be glad to vote that wattage to KFBK.

But Carlos had to *prove* KFBK better served the "public interest" than the station whose frequency and wattage it targeted for takeover.

In the case of KFBK, one of the stations it considered as a takeover target was KFSG in Los Angeles, the station of nationally known evangelist Aimee Semple McPherson. The exclusively religious programming could be considered a violation of the public interest standard because it did not meet the criteria of appeal to a diverse audience.[78]

But Carlos McClatchy's petition for greater signal strength and consideration over KFSG was unsuccessful. The small station in Sacramento serving a general audience was unable to successfully prove its "public interest" value against a powerful, high-profile broadcast radio station in Los Angeles owned by a media celebrity and serving only its congregants and the star-struck.

It would be 1935 before KFBK would get a boost in broadcast power to five thousand watts.[79]

So by the end of 1928, KFBK had been reassigned to 1,310 kilocycles and remained at one hundred watts of power. Seeking perhaps to make broadcast lemonade out of regulatory lemons, a *Sacramento Bee* article pronounced the 1928 Davis Amendment–driven frequency reallocations "far from perfect" but "excellent" in basic principle. The article also highlighted programming changes that year, including the arrival of East Coast radio programs to Pacific coast listeners courtesy of NBC and the launch of the new Columbia Broadcasting System (CBS).[80]

But Kimball-Upson apparently had had enough, and on November 9, 1928, it sent a written declaration of intent to give up its interest in the station to W.H. James of the *Sacramento Bee*. The buyout requested by Kimball-Upson? $12,500.[81]

POISED FOR EXPANSION

The McClatchy Company survived the unstable regulatory environment and entered what is known as the "Golden Age of Radio" in the 1930s as sole owners of KFBK. In addition to the company's flagship Sacramento property and the 1925 purchase of KMJ in Fresno, Carlos McClatchy continued to direct resources into expanding the broadcasting arm of the family's holdings and enhancing the value of the existing broadcast properties. In 1930, the McClatchy Company purchased KWG in Stockton, the station whose previous owner had attempted to encroach into the McClatchys' broadcast territory just two years before. The company also purchased KSMR in Santa Maria; that station's license was moved to Bakersfield, and the call letters changed to KERN.[82]

Having no intention of staying within the borders of California, Carlos McClatchy's most ambitious broadcasting expansion project was the 1931 acquisition of Reno, Nevada station KOH following almost two years of negotiations and FRC hearings.[83]

McClatchy-owned companies now held broadcast as well as print media in Sacramento and Fresno, a radio station in Stockton, the major newspaper in Modesto, a radio station in Bakersfield and a radio station in Reno, Nevada. By 1931, McClatchy companies were controlling the primary media throughout California's Central Valley from Sacramento in the north to Bakersfield in the south.

The McClatchy home (above) on Twenty-second Street is now the Ella K. McClatchy Branch of the Sacramento Public Library (opposite). *Center for Sacramento History*.

In 1931, *Sacramento Bee* business manager G.C. Hamilton responded to an inquiry from the *Bridgeport Herald* in Connecticut about the newspaper's experience in owning radio stations. "Both the Sacramento and the Fresno stations are profitable, and while we do not know that it has increased newspaper linage, we do feel that they are builders of prestige and as such are a great help in maintaining and holding circulation." While acknowledging that the *Sacramento Bee* and the *Fresno Bee* were in the newspaper business and focused on building newspaper advertising "to the exclusion of everything else," he also stated an unusual point of view for a newspaper. His recognition that there were "some accounts for which radio is more desirable than newspapers" and admission that he would not hesitate to sell a client only radio if that were what the client wished showed an understanding that radio was more than an adjunct to the newspapers. Radio was a separate medium and served a separate constituency, admittedly with some crossover with the newspaper's readership. "We do not believe in high-powered radio stations," Hamilton told the *Bridgeport Herald*.[84] The audience was local and, as such, had local needs that had to be addressed, something national network programming could only partially accomplish.

In addition to station acquisition, the McClatchy Company enhanced its broadcast program offerings by becoming part of the CBS chain. A front-page article in the *Bee* the day before the inaugural broadcast stoked listeners' excitement, promising programs Sacramentans could not hear on any other station in the region. The new programming originated from New York, Chicago and other producing studios in the CBS chain of broadcasting affiliates.[85]

The CBS hook-up was a key selling point for the advertising departments of *Bee*-owned stations KFBK, KWG and KMJ. As far as *Sacramento Bee* business manager G.C. Hamilton knew, these three stations were the only one-hundred-watt radio stations in the country on the CBS chain. In addition to the CBS affiliation, these three *Bee* radio stations were also affiliated with West Coast chain Don Lee Broadcasting. Listeners in and around Sacramento were estimated at about 100,000, and advertising could be purchased on all three stations in combination, providing, as Hamilton put it, coverage "of the interior valleys of the state from fifty miles north of Sacramento to fifty miles south of Fresno, a distance of two hundred and seventy-five miles in length, and approximately fifty miles in width."[86]

4

LISTENING IN AND TALKING BACK

There is one thing every capital city should have, and this is a radio station. Sacramento has it—a good one too. Clear as a bell, always. Another thing that is of credit to this station is the—what? The radio announcers. The silver voiced announcers—ah—they are fine—honest.
—Elmo Griffith, 1930

KFBK listener and Auburn, California resident Elmo Griffith was so enamored of the station, its programs and its announcers that he practically insisted on station entry. "Next time I come down to Sacramento I would like to come into KFBK and take a look at one of those announcers…if you will not let me in you will have to hire me to sing. I must see those announcers."[87]

Radio broadcasting was not point-to-point communication like the telephone. Listeners received the broadcasts—an announcer's voice entering their homes—but those same listeners could not comment to the voice, interject or get a response in real time. No actual "relationship" existed between the voice on the radio that entered the intimate domestic space and the listener in the home, although some listeners attempted to fashion the listening experience into something more personal. Fan mail and criticism—sometimes addressed to the radio station in general, sometimes to the station manager and sometimes to no one in particular—represented for the listener a way of "talking back" to the radio.[88] Members of the public could not take to the airwaves themselves, but they could, on a much smaller scale, be heard by those whose voices came into their own homes.

C.K. McClatchy (left) with longtime friend, California governor and U.S. senator Hiram Johnson, circa 1930. *Center for Sacramento History.*

Elmo Griffith was very direct in stating his desire to see the announcers. Another "active" listener, Dora Hoernlein of Woodland, California, was much less forceful than Griffith but no less ardent in her desire to visit the studio to see the announcers whose voices entered her home. "We often motor to Sacramento and many times I have wanted to visit your studio, but could not force myself to do so," she admitted somewhat shyly.[89] For the vast majority of Americans, this was the sum total of their interaction with the public airwaves. They could listen and they could write in, but they would never be on the air.

By 1930, an estimated 52,581,680 people made up the total U.S. radio audience, and 43 percent of American families owned a radio. Among these people, the average length of listening time was three hours and seven minutes per day on the Pacific coast and slightly less than three hours per day east of the Rocky Mountains.[90] Radio had grown so much and so rapidly that even "radio-phobic" C.K. McClatchy recognized its importance. In the 1930 census, the first census to ask if there was a radio in the home, C.K. and Ella McClatchy are logged in the report as owning a radio.[91] Where he had not even owned a radio two years previously, he now felt inclined to offer his longtime friend Senator Hiram Johnson advice on Johnson's radio delivery in an effort to make the senator more appealing to listeners.[92] At this time, KFBK was on the air daily from 4:30 p.m. to 11:00 p.m. with an added morning broadcast schedule on Fridays from 10:00 a.m. to 1:30 p.m. Since the McClatchy stations were affiliated with both the CBS and Don Lee Broadcasting chains, listeners were assured national-quality programming even though the McClatchy stations' power remained at only one hundred watts.[93]

A STRANGELY INTIMATE RELATIONSHIP

By this time, broadcast radio had assumed an important position in American popular culture. For many Americans the local station—or the nearest station they could receive—was a significant part of their daily lives. Voices broadcast from the studio and entering the home gave some listeners a false sense of a "relationship" where none actually existed. Announcers were celebrities and the announcers on national broadcasts were famous across the country. More and more, radio came to be about a shared, homogenized experience provided by national network programs and less about the voices of individuals and ethnic, racial or shared interest groups. And as radio grew in importance in people's daily lives, the business of radio became more profitable for those who, like the McClatchys, were able to leverage their early entry into the medium and who successfully weathered the chaotic period of the FRC's signal reallocation.

For listeners during the Depression, what they heard regularly on the radio provided something of a sense of community as so much of their world was in a state of flux. The upheaval created by the economic crisis changed the most basic elements of their daily lives—work, housing, food and what little security they might have had.[94] A new sense of community developed for listeners who began to use radio as a way to adapt to America's new mass culture and redefine their changing world in more familiar ways. For some listeners who tried to "talk back," like Elmo Griffith and Dora Hoernlein, this meant creating these new kinds of relationships with the people they heard on the air.[95]

Not all "talking back" by the public was complimentary, of course.

As already noted, when the vague "public interest" standard was established in the Radio Act of 1927, the airwaves were legislated a scarce public resource. Station owners and broadcasters who were allowed the use of this public resource were expected to reflect the general interests of the audience, not serve as a vehicle for the station owner's personal opinions.[96] If the "public interest, convenience and necessity" standard was undefined for broadcasters, then it was most certainly vague for the listening public. What listeners sometimes failed to understand was that this standard was a two-way street. Just as broadcasters could not use the airwaves to promote their own special interests, listeners and advertisers could not use the airwaves as a weapon to make a direct attack on an individual or a competing company.

When Lucy A. Bishop of the International Bible Students Association (IBSA) threatened to petition the FRC to revoke the license of the

McClatchy station on the grounds that the station wished to "prevent people from hearing the truth"—the programs produced by the IBSA—the IBSA representative justified her cause with her own version of the public interest standard in response to what she heard on the air from those with whom she did not agree:

> *The people of the land are entitled to the truth…The law says that stations should broadcast that which is of public interest, convenience and necessity. These programs* [of the IBSA] *come clearly within this provision. It is a necessity for the people to have the truth. It is convenient for them to have the truth because it builds them up in the right way. It is of public interest because it shows the people the reason for the present depressed times and what is the remedy.*

McClatchy business manager G.C. Hamilton responded to Lucy Bishop with his own brief lesson in what constituted the public interest. Informing her that the news and advertising policy for KFBK mirrored that of the *Sacramento Bee*, he stated:

> *It has always been a matter of policy with us that no advertising would be permitted which was a direct attack upon somebody else and contentious in character. We only allow that advertising which is for the direct purpose of promoting the business of the client, and always forbid an attempt to tear down a competitor…We do not attempt to pass upon the merits of any proposition, and do not accept that which forces us into this position.*[97]

Active radio listeners—those who comfortably and perhaps regularly wrote to their local radio station, participated in station write-in contests and offered feedback on programs—were radio's grass-roots level. They also provided radio's saleable commodity—an identifiable audience. And the more that audience "talked back," the more it could be measured and sold to advertisers. If a local business could be shown, through accumulated letters and postcards, the geographic range of listeners to the local station, that local business would have a justification for advertising on the local station or sponsoring a local program. A 1930 survey asked radio listeners how they express their appreciation of programs presented by stations and companies. Of listeners polled on the Pacific coast, 37 percent said they purchased the products mentioned. For the country as a whole, 26 percent responded that they showed their appreciation by purchasing the advertiser's product.[98]

THE IMPACT OF SIGNAL REALLOCATION

By 1930, the extensive, and in some cases multiple, frequency reassignments endured by stations in the wake of the Radio Act of 1927 resulted in the shuttering of hundreds of small stations that had lost their licenses or gone out of business.[99] KFBK and the other McClatchy radio stations, however, successfully navigated the FRC's multiple frequency reassignments. And although Carlos McClatchy's 1928 request to boost KFBK's power proved unsuccessful, the one-hundred-watt station maintained its importance because of its Don Lee and CBS network affiliations, which in turn strengthened the audience it could offer to advertisers. While a number of newspapers across the country ceased their radio operations during the late 1920s—citing the costliness of running a broadcast station as the primary reason—McClatchy newspapers continued to expand their radio holdings. In the midst of the Depression, both KFBK in Sacramento and KMJ in Fresno, the company's two longest-established radio stations, were profitable.[100] This mindset and business operation is what set McClatchy newspapers apart and resulted in a different broadcasting experience than their newspaper counterparts across the country. It is unknown if the

Carlos McClatchy was a respected and influential journalist in his own right. *Seated, left to right*: newspaperman George Wect and Governor Hiram Johnson; *standing, left to right*: Edward Dickson, L.A. Express; Alex McCabe, secretary to Hiram Johnson; Archibald Johnson, the governor's son; Charles St. Clair, Associated Press correspondent; and Carlos McClatchy. Image circa 1912–14. *Center for Sacramento History*.

operation of the radio stations increased the advertising space sold in either the Sacramento or the Fresno newspapers, but the McClatchy Company regarded the radio stations as "builders of prestige and…a great help in maintaining and holding circulation."[101]

Carlos McClatchy was certainly an innovator when it came to viewing broadcast radio as a valid medium in its own right and as a valuable asset to a newspaper publishing company. But for his part, William Randolph Hearst was just beginning to assert his presence in radio broadcasting. It had been an uphill fight for Hearst as he spent years convincing reluctant publishers to invest in radio stations and in radio as a promotional vehicle for their publications. "I would like to make a definite declaration that in my opinion every newspaper in our service ought to own at least a controlling interest in a radio station, either by purchase or by long lease. If this cannot be accomplished through the purchase of one of the best existing stations, it may be necessary for the paper to build a station of its own," Hearst noted.[102]

By this time, all of the McClatchy stations were part of the CBS chain and the Don Lee Broadcasting System. Although operating at only one hundred watts of power, the Sacramento, Fresno and Stockton stations were able to provide national programs to their local audiences. As the McClatchy newspaper and radio holdings grew to multiple newspapers and stations in separate local communities, the two media—newspapers and broadcast radio—were being viewed more and more by their parent company as separate business operations. Newspaper owners who also owned radio stations tended to view their stations as a way to enhance the image of their papers and to build newspaper circulation and advertising linage sold; the McClatchy Company, however, saw its radio stations as serving an audience distinct from the newspaper readership, even if listeners were also readers.

NBC AND THE FORMATION OF THE DON LEE BROADCASTING SYSTEM

Network—or chain—broadcasting is the simultaneous broadcast of an identical program on two or more connected stations. The program was transmitted by wire, typically in the form of a leased telephone line, from the point of the program's origin to each affiliate station on the chain for concurrent broadcasting.[103] NBC, the first national network, was established in 1926; CBS was established the following year, in 1927. Close on the heels of these national networks came regional chains, like the Don Lee Broadcasting System, that sought to link together radio stations to serve smaller regions rather than to serve the entire country.

The McClatchy connection with the Don Lee Broadcasting System began early. The Don Lee chain, one of the earliest regional networks in the country, was established in December 1928, when Don Lee, Inc., a Bay Area automobile dealer, connected its San Francisco radio station, KFRC, and its Los Angeles station, KHJ, via telephone circuit.[104] McClatchy's three stations—KFBK in Sacramento, KMJ in Fresno and KWG in Stockton—joined the Don Lee chain within its first month of operations, making the McClatchy Company among the first to sign on to this new concept—the regional radio network.[105] NBC had only recently reached the West Coast with its programming when it established the Pacific Coast network with stations in San Francisco, Oakland, Los Angeles, Portland, Spokane and Seattle. And at that, NBC was unsure if it would be able to link its stations in the East and the Midwest with the Pacific Coast network for the April 5, 1927 inaugural coast-to-coast broadcast.[106]

The importance of Don Lee to McClatchy radio lay in the access to national programming. Through the Don Lee affiliation, KFBK, KMJ and KWG carried CBS network programming beginning in 1930, allowing the low-powered one-hundred-watt McClatchy stations to carry national programs despite broadcast limits. Although CBS, under the leadership of William Paley, had made strides in developing as a national network, NBC was still dominant. It was only through the association with Don Lee's chain that CBS was truly able to be national.[107] At this time, Greater Sacramento–area residents able to tune in to KFBK could also likely tune in to KGO in Oakland, whose broadcast schedules the *Bee* carried in its radio section, and listen to NBC network programs. The Don Lee hook-up and CBS affiliation gave Sacramento listeners a choice and provided national programs to Fresno and Stockton listeners as well. On a single evening, Sacramento listeners would have the option of hearing, for example, *Guy Lombardo's Orchestra* on KFBK, *Amos 'n' Andy* on KGO, *Cecil and Sally* on KPO or *Black and Blue* on KFRC.[108]

According to NBC executives, however, network broadcasting was not a profitable enterprise in spite of the intense interest shown in linking the country coast to coast. In 1927, just eight months after NBC inaugurated its Pacific Coast network, making it truly a "national" network, NBC president Merlin H. Aylesworth testified before the Federal Trade Commission as part of the commission's inquiry into the operation of RCA, the parent company of NBC. At the hearing in 1927, Aylesworth testified that NBC had lost money since its formation and that the company had not "broken even" since its organization. According to Aylesworth, the three corporations that controlled NBC—RCA, General Electric and Westinghouse Electric—were compensated "indirectly by reason of an increased public interest and the consequent increased consumption of radio sets and accessories."[109] In other words, although national broadcasting was not a profitable enterprise in and of itself, the resultant sales of radio sets, broadcasting equipment and other components did result in profitable business.

But if networks were not profitable, NBC certainly appeared to be investing a lot in them for very little return.

5

"I DO NOT KNOW WHAT IN THE NAME OF GOD TO DO"

The Argonne fighting was our infantry against the Boche [German] *artillery and his machine guns and snipers. We saw little of his infantry, though we were praying for that chance. Instead, hundreds of machine guns, hidden in trenches or concealed in the many woods covered every inch of our approach. The snipers were everywhere. When we went through woods, German snipers would stay concealed, opening up on our backs after we were through. Several of them selected me for their special targets when I was out on particular missions, but they proved bad shots.*

—*Carlos McClatchy, 1918*[110]

In the summer of 1920 at the age of twenty-nine, Carlos McClatchy ran the editorial side of the *Sacramento Bee* while his father, C.K.; mother, Ella; and sister Eleanor embarked on a twenty-two-month trip through North Africa, the Mediterranean and western Europe.[111]

Like his father, Carlos was a strong personality, a respected journalist and a man used to being in charge. He ran things his way. Carlos made the controversial decision to publish a graphic image on the front page of the December 10, 1920 edition of the *Sacramento Bee* showing the lynching of three "gangsters" jailed for killing three police officers. The men had been dragged from their Santa Rosa jail cell and hanged in the early morning hours of December 10. The photograph that ran in the *Bee* had been taken by flashlight at the scene of the hanging and then immediately sent by airplane to Sacramento's Mather Field so Carlos could run the image that same day on the front page.[112]

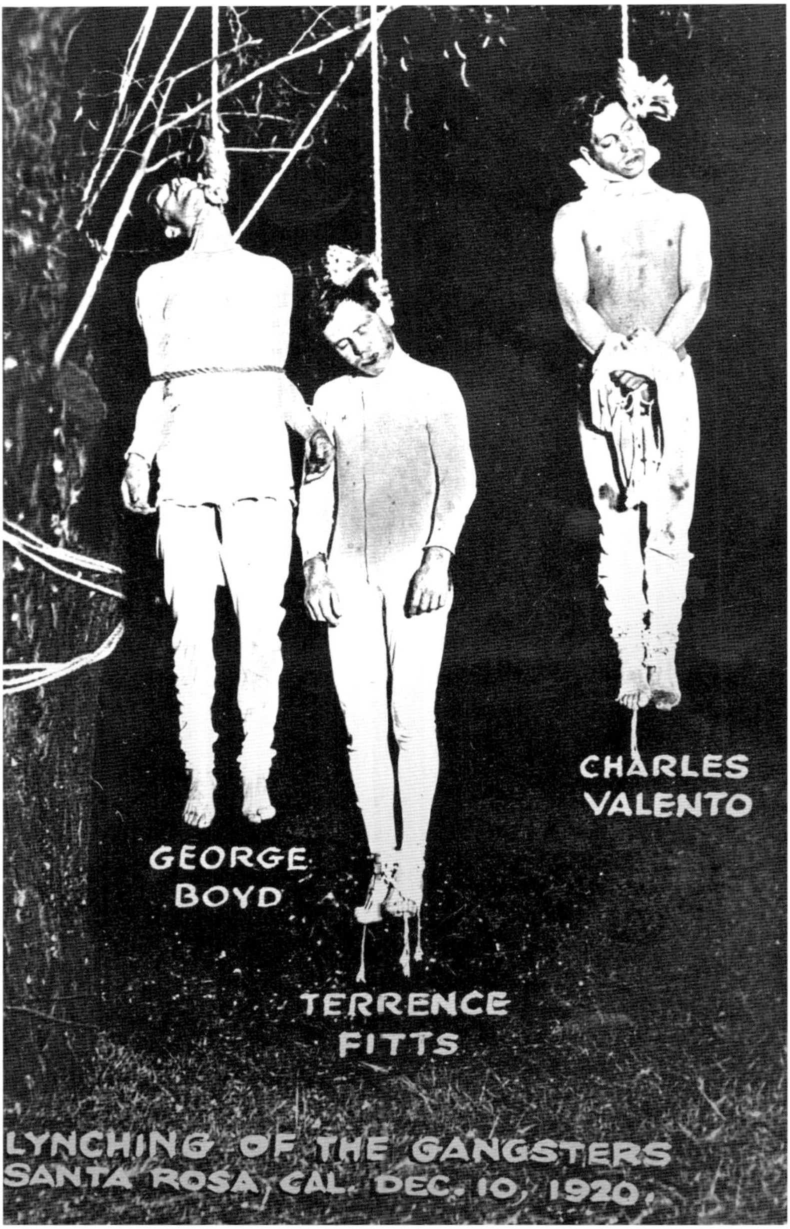

In 1920, Carlos McClatchy ran this graphic image of three men lynched by a mob in Santa Rosa on the front page of the *Sacramento Bee*, attracting condemnation from advertisers and other newspaper publishers. *Center for Sacramento History*.

That very edition of the *Bee*, however, also included a Christmas advertisement from Sacramento department store Weinstock-Lubin & Co. The advertisement was an invitation to Sacramento children to attend a doll reception at the department store hosted by Santa Claus and Goldilocks. The store's board of directors was furious. In protest, Weinstock-Lubin ran an "apology" ad in the *Sacramento Bee*, the *Sacramento Star* and the *Sacramento Union* that said, in part:

> *In our desire to reach the public, we strive to have our advertisements enter the homes of the city. Realizing that we cannot be successful in achieving this if the media we use are unclean or unwholesome, we have, from time to time, protested to the papers if they placed undesirable matter in the same issue in which our advertisements appeared…Our advertisement in the* Evening Bee *of last Friday was a special appeal to children. On the front page of the same issue there was published a photograph of a lynching—one of the most horrible pictures we have ever seen in any newspaper. We feel that no child should have seen that picture, and we regret that in appealing to the children of the city we were probably instrumental in increasing the number of those who were subjected to such a gross indignity.*[113]

Carlos accepted the ad for publication in the *Bee*, giving Weinstock-Lubin the opportunity to present its side, but in that same edition, he ran an editorial that left no doubt that advertisers do not control the editorial content of the *Bee*. Even the newspaper's largest advertisers did not determine the news. Carlos, a veteran of the Great War, noted that "pictures of far more ghastly subjects were published during the war." In addition, other newspapers that had piped up in criticism of the lynching photograph, Carlos noted, "ran in all its gory details the picture of the bomb outrage on Wall Street [referring to the September 16, 1920 bombing that killed thirty-eight and injured more than one hundred others], the scene of thirty bodies mangled and spattered on the surrounding walls." He drove the point home:

> *This department store, which has departments ranging from millinery to pins, through departments of How to Run A City, What's Wrong With Sacramento, and the Do As I Say department, seems now to have added another on Newspaper Censorship. Weinstock-Lubin as a commercial store is an efficient institution. Sacramento, however, has declined with thanks the invitation for her affairs to be run by that store and evaded with difficulty the attempts to do so.*[114]

Carlos McClatchy was tough, stubborn, brilliant and in desperate need to be his own man. Getting out from under the control of parents, C.K. and Ella, however, proved to be difficult. C.K. persisted in holding the reins in Carlos's professional life, and Ella tried to maintain a tight grip on her son's personal life. Carlos chafed at both.

Originally, Carlos was to be named Charles—just as his father C.K. was Charles Kenny—but Ella McClatchy, who held more of a firm hand on the family than previously thought, said she would have "no more 'Charlies' around the house." She named her only son Carlos and gave him the middle name "Kelly" for her family name. In fact later, when Carlos and his wife, Phebe, named their son "Charles Kenny" after his grandfather, Ella became very angry—not just about the use of "Charles" but also about the name "Kenny" instead of "Kelly." "She said that Kenny didn't mean anything," Phebe McClatchy later recalled. "It was just the name of an old priest that they put in there. She was so indignant but it was too late. We had named the baby after his grandfather."[115]

One can assume that Ella was used to getting her way, and it is evident she tried to exert control over Carlos and Phebe from the beginning. Even in her own life, Ella exerted control over perceptions of her, resorting to a long-standing fabrication that she was born on the day of Abraham Lincoln's inauguration as president rather than a year before the inauguration, as becomes clear when one examines the census records. The fact that Ella and C.K. married on February 12, Lincoln's birthday, leant another layer to the contrived connection between Ella McClatchy and Abraham Lincoln.

By contrast, Carlos's bride was from the Briggs and Rideout families, both prominent, moneyed, cultured families in the Marysville area.

CARLOS AND PHEBE

Phebe's family, the Briggses, knew the McClatchys, although the two families were not close. Phebe certainly did not know Carlos growing up. As she put it, "He was away at college while I was at home, and when he came home, I was away." However, as a child she did know Carlos's younger sister, Eleanor.

By all accounts, Carlos was brilliant. For Ella McClatchy, her son was her pride and joy. After he completed his early schooling in Sacramento, he went to Santa Clara to attend Christian Brothers College. "She [Ella] didn't think it was good enough for him and in fact he wanted to do something better, but his father said it was good enough for his brother and for Hiram Johnson and it was good enough for Carlos," Phebe said. But Ella, not to be deterred, managed to get Carlos into Columbia University, over the protests of C.K.[116] The agreement was that if Carlos worked hard and finished at Columbia in three years, he could have one year in Europe. Carlos's years at Columbia University proved to be both exciting and eye opening. It was a new world for him. "He was never again provincial," Phebe said. But instead of touring Europe at the end of his three years at Columbia, he was called back to Sacramento by his father. The needs of the *Bee* superseded any other commitment, and C.K. and the *Bee* needed Carlos.[117]

Carlos McClatchy in uniform, circa 1918. During the Great War, Carlos earned a battlefield promotion to captain. *Center for Sacramento History.*

Carlos would not get to Europe until the U.S. Army sent him there as a soldier in the Great War.

As a "lively and fearless reporter," Carlos knew what was going on everywhere in Sacramento, and he was liked and trusted by many different types of people. It was during this period—in 1916—when he met Phebe Briggs, who at the time was in her senior year at Vassar College. Her recounting of how they met speaks both to Carlos's skill as a reporter and the intellectual foundation of their relationship. Phebe was writing a thesis for an economics seminar, and her father introduced her to Carlos as someone who would be a valuable resource in her research:

> *I was to research the I.W.W.* [Industrial Workers of the World], *or "Wobblies," as they were called. They had been active on the West Coast, had been burning ranches up and down the valley, and had even attacked some elements in the towns. In Sacramento they were driven out by fire hoses. Carlos had been in the midst of their activities and could take me to the leaders in their hidden headquarters, where we discussed their theories and their problems. As a result, I produced a good thesis. Carlos and I became friends after I returned from College. His vitality and charm made the other young men seem dull. His mind was amazingly quick.*[118]

Phebe, who was Phi Beta Kappa and graduated *cum laude* from Vassar College in 1916, seemed the perfect match for the innovative, energetic and brilliant Carlos. Their romance—and in particular their wedding—did not sit well with everyone, however, and even sparked a few hard feelings.

With the United States entering the "war in Europe," as World War I was known at the time, Carlos went into the army and was stationed at Camp Lewis—now Fort Lewis—in Tacoma, Washington, for final training before shipping out to Europe. Phebe Briggs and her mother visited him at the camp. Perhaps the biggest surprise that came out of that visit was the decision to marry before Carlos shipped out. The January 13, 1918 telegram Carlos sent his mother, Ella McClatchy, must have been quite a shock (punctuation has been added for clarity):

> *PHEBE AND I ENGAGED. PLANS TO BE MARRIED THIS SATURDAY. THOUGH A HARD TRIP I WANT YOU AND FAMILY TO BE HERE EVER SO MUCH. IF POSSIBLE DATE IMPOSSIBLE WILL CHANGE IT. JUST DECIDED ALL THIS SO COULDN'T LET YOU KNOW BEFORE. I KNOW CK AND YOU WILL LIKE YOUR NEW DAUGHTER. ANSWER DAY WIRE. PLEASE KEEP CONFIDENTIAL. BEST LOVE. ANSWER DAY TELEGRAM*
> *CARLOS*[119]

As Phebe recalled, there was no time to waste and the wedding had to be simple. Ella McClatchy was not pleased at the arrangements—or lack thereof. Phebe said:

> *I discovered Carlos's mother was not coming, and the reason was that we had not planned to be married by a priest. Carlos had no preference in the matter since he had already abandoned, and been abandoned by, his mother's church. It seemed important to me that she should participate in the wedding of her only son on the eve of his going to war, so we decided to have a priest, a dispensation was arranged, and his parents came. We were married in Seattle, in a hotel, in January, 1918. There were seeds of trouble, though I was too innocent, or too stupid, to detect them. When my grandmother* [Phebe Rideout] *heard of the priest, she cancelled her reservations, and changed her will, leaving me out of what was then a large fortune.*

Phebe Briggs married Carlos McClatchy during the Great War, just before he was sent to Europe. She is seen here with one of their three sons. *Center for Sacramento History.*

Eventually, however, Phebe's grandmother—for whom she was named, right down to the unusual spelling—grew to love Carlos, which put the younger Phebe back in the good graces of the elder Phebe.[120]

During the war, Carlos was in the Argonne Forest along the western front, scene of some of the worst fighting. As Phebe recounted later, most of the men in his outfit were killed. Carlos wrote in a letter to his mother-in-law while he was in Belgium that "our losses were more than I risk censorship in telling. Many of my best friends in the regiment are dead; many more wounded. Few of us are left, after the remainder went to the hospital for exhaustion."[121]

Ironically, Carlos—who would be instrumental in bringing radio broadcasting technology to the West Coast a mere three years later—was routinely under shell-fire because radio technology was not available on the battlefield. As information officer, Carlos ran back and forth from the front lines to the command post with news from the front and orders from command. As he wrote to his mother-in-law:

> *For eight days we had no blankets nor hot food. All the time we were out in the open, under continuous shell fire that exacted its daily toll in dead and mangled. But the regiment fought wonderfully, achieved a wide fame for itself, was cited in orders, and now, but a skeleton of its former self, but refilled with recruits and new officers, is about to take another whack at the Boches* [German soldiers].[122]

Carlos came out fifteen pounds underweight and with a battlefield promotion to captain. He wrote to his mother-in-law:

> *I earned it, for many a time I thought there wasn't a single chance of seeing my Phebe again. The Colonel tells everybody I was under more shell-fire than anyone in the regiment, and I certainly know I had my share, for I went forward with each advance, and in addition was out on special missions that kept me exposed to shell-fire, machine gun barrages and snipers, a combination of these feats with the attack on Gesnes* [France] *leading to the recommendation for gallantry.*

He enclosed the order from the commander in chief for his battlefield promotion, proud to be able to offer it to Phebe.[123]

While Carlos was at war, Phebe worked in Washington in the personnel office of the War Department. She headed a section that assigned draftees

This wartime photograph taken in Belgium in 1918 shows (left to right) Lee Sumnet, "Joffre" Weil, Carlos McClatchy and Earley Granger. *Center for Sacramento History.*

to their overseas units, trying to place men in positions for which they were qualified. Because of the difficulties of wartime she received few letters from Carlos while in Washington. "Every day on my way to work I passed the casualty office, where the casualties of the day before were posted," she said. "His name was never listed, and he came home alive but badly worn by his experiences."[124]

One would guess his wartime experiences also made him less inclined to accept being pushed around, especially by his own family.

Upon returning from the war, Carlos and Phebe settled in Sacramento, and Carlos went to work for the *Bee*. It was during this period that he brought the idea of broadcast radio to C.K. and established KVQ.

It was also at this time that Carlos went on the first of his drinking binges—what Phebe referred to as his "devastating sprees." Carlos disappeared, and it was Phebe's brother who found him and brought him home, where Phebe nursed and comforted him.[125]

CARLOS AND C.K.

In 1922, Carlos took an opportunity to strike out on his own. The same year he convinced his father to involve the company in the new medium of radio, Carlos became editor of the newly established *Fresno Bee*. Unfortunately, C.K. was as strong willed as his son, and he insisted on micromanaging Carlos's operation and dictating the Fresno paper's position on the issues from his Sacramento office.[126] Carlos was required to stay in close touch with his father and traveled back and forth to Sacramento once a week

But family involvement began to be interminable for Carlos. Not only was his father attempting to manage the editorial stance of the Fresno paper, but Carlos had also been forced to accept one cousin as business manager and another cousin as circulation manager. Carlos had personally supervised all aspects of the *Fresno Bee*'s establishment, from buying the equipment and hiring the staff to forging relationships with Fresno-area businesses and potential advertisers, and this family arrangement angered him.[127] When C.K. and his brother, Valentine (V.S.), became bitterly divided and C.K. bought V.S. out of any control of the *Bee* publications, Carlos's cousins—the sons of V.S.—also left the papers.[128]

It is said that there were such hard feelings between C.K. and V.S., that when the two brothers met on San Francisco's Market Street in 1924, V.S. refused C.K.'s outstretched hand. Six months later, when Eleanor got married, she returned a wedding gift from her uncle unopened. Her note to V.S. read, "As you refuse to have friendly relations with my father, you can, of course, understand my not wishing to accept your gift, no matter how kindly intended."[129]

This episode also left bad feelings for Phebe Briggs McClatchy's family.

"C.K. and his brother V.S. disagreed and they had a contest as to which would acquire the *Bee*…It was a bidding contest, and each one tried to get as much money loaned to them as they could," Phebe recalled. "Neither of them had large amounts of money themselves. C.K. had run the paper, but he had never taken profits out of it. In fact, I don't suppose there were an awful lot of profits. It was well-run, it was respected and V.S. was a good businessman on the business side. They ran a remarkable paper, but they didn't make a remarkable amount of money."[130]

According to Phebe McClatchy, her parents were devoted to Carlos and had great respect for him. Phebe's grandmother Phebe Rideout was the widow of a banker and was prepared to help fund the buyout of V.S. McClatchy for the sake of Carlos, not out of any concern for either C.K. or Ella. Phebe Rideout gave $80,000 and the Briggses, Phebe McClatchy's parents, came up with another $20,000. Carlos's wife's family turned over $100,000 for C.K. to use in buying out V.S., who went on to establish a real estate and insurance business. "But [the McClatchys] were very resentful and wouldn't speak to us," Phebe said. "It always hurt me and my mother that the McClatchy family never acknowledged the Rideouts and Briggs provided the extra money that enabled C.K. to buy out V.S." As Phebe noted, her parents did it for Carlos, whom they admired and trusted. And while the money was paid back, Eleanor—Carlos's sister who would one day take over operation of the McClatchy media holdings upon C.K.'s death—never would say anything about the help…a slight that hurt her sister-in-law Phebe deeply.[131]

Valentine Stuart (V.S.) McClatchy, C.K. McClatchy's brother, was a partner in the newspapers at one time. Ultimately, the two brothers rarely spoke to one another. *Center for Sacramento History*.

After receiving financial assistance from Carlos's in-laws for the buyout, C.K. still attempted to oversee the Fresno operation and manage his son's business affairs.

Not only was Carlos unable to wrest full control from his father, but he also knew that under the present terms of C.K.'s will, he would one day have to share control of the newspapers and radio stations with his sisters, Charlotte and Eleanor, neither of whom had ever worked in the publishing or broadcasting business. "I haven't the slightest interest in pledging my lifework so that larger and larger sums could be made by the *Bee* so two-thirds of its revenues would be spent in idle luxury. Life is too short, the work is too hard, the motive too futile."[132]

Fighting C.K. on the financial arrangement involving his siblings, Carlos managed to succeed in reaching an agreement with C.K. by which Carlos alone would inherit the newspapers and, presumably, the broadcasting side of the business. Carlos's mother, Ella, would receive a guaranteed annual income from the *Bee* enterprises, and his sisters, Charlotte and Eleanor, would be given very substantial trust funds. With the issue settled, Carlos began to work toward fulfilling his vision of building a media empire. Only thirty-three at this time, he set to work eliminating the competition

Carlos McClatchy with one of his three sons. *Center for Sacramento History*.

of the Fresno paper by buying a Modesto, California newspaper and buying or creating radio stations throughout California's Central Valley and Nevada's Reno area, and he had plans in the offing to purchase or start newspapers in Bakersfield, San Jose, San Diego, Santa Barbara and Phoenix, Arizona.[133] The reins were held so tightly by the Sacramento office, however, that Carlos lost at least one important business deal because of the control. "Very many times Carlos would have ideas," Phebe said. "He would want to do something new—and it got squelched."[134]

One deal that was killed was the purchase of the Santa Barbara newspaper from the Storks.

"Carlos knew the head of that famous Santa Barbara paper," Phebe remembered. "Mr. Stork had in mind to sell, and Carlos was in touch with the newspaper and with Mr. Stork, and he went back and forth." Carlos wanted to buy the paper, Phebe said, and Stork wanted to sell to the *Bee*. "But C.K. put his foot down [and] wouldn't let him go on with it. And that was a big disappointment for Carlos. I don't think anybody else knew about it," Phebe said. "It was just in the family."[135]

In spite of these challenges, Carlos displayed tremendous vision and a drive and work ethic to rival that of his father. Unfortunately, like his father, Carlos was also a hard drinker. But where heavy drinking did not appear to have ill effects for C.K., for Carlos, it was devastating.

CARLOS AND THE BOTTLE

According to Phebe, Carlos's drinking began at an early age—when he was in high school. At that time, the *Bee* was not terribly prosperous, and Carlos was expected to work over his summer break. He went down to the waterfront and worked with the stevedores.

He also learned to drink with the stevedores.

By the time he and Phebe were married, he already had a serious drinking problem. Shortly after their marriage, Phebe and Carlos had a discussion about his drinking:

> *He said, "If you want me to, I'll say right now that I'll never take another drink." I didn't have any sense; if I'd accepted that, he could have stopped then. But I said, "I don't want* [you] *to do that; I trust you to do what you think best." He didn't stop, you see—he could have stopped then, at least I think he could have if he'd wanted to. But later he couldn't, and it was too late. He had already gotten into a bad habit and something of a bad name for drinking before we were married and I just ignored it.*[136]

By 1932, Carlos's drinking was of tremendous concern, and his behavior began to cast doubt on his ability to one day assume control of the entire McClatchy operation. His drinking resulted in bizarre incidents of behavior that did not escape public notice, and C.K. was at a loss. "I do not know what in the name of God to do," C.K. wrote to Hiram Johnson. "He is a wonderful newspaperman and he has done wonderful work on the papers. But he spoils it all by his periods of practical craziness which have become notorious here in Sacramento, in Fresno, and probably in San Francisco—periods in which he does the most outlandish things and says the wildest things and says them to anybody and everybody who will listen."[137]

According to C.K., Carlos was beginning to be "dictatorial" and obstinate. Expressing that he will leave the McClatchy papers and find work elsewhere "if things do not go his way," it is unclear in this instance how much of the difficulty is related to his drinking and how much is related to frustration over C.K.'s inability to relinquish control of the editorial policies of the *Fresno Bee*.[138]

It appears, though, that the drinking was in the back of the family's mind as the situation progressed. Ella expressed concern to C.K. about the safety of the newspapers, Carlos's safety, her safety and the safety of the children. Presumably she meant her grandchildren but possibly also her daughters, who had a financial stake in the business operations as well. In his frustration, C.K. explained to Hiram Johnson that Carlos had taken a short "treatment" and that there were hopes it would set him "on the right road," but it seemed to have had no effect. C.K. doubted that Carlos could be convinced to undertake such treatment again.[139]

Business relationships were beginning to be impacted. While "not himself" and under the care of nurses for a three-week period in his family's

Sacramento home when C.K. was in China, Carlos was "telephoning all the time to everybody telling all his business and the business of the *Bee*." Carlos went so far as to tell someone to go buy votes for the Silver Creek Project water bond measure and that the *Bee* would reimburse him for his efforts, telling the man "there wasn't a mean, low, dirty, nasty thing the *Bee* would not do in order to win the election. He denies all that, but every word of it is true because everybody in the house heard him roaring," C.K. wrote to his friend.[140]

The situation worsened to the point that C.K. had apparently asked Hiram to intervene. In a conversation with Hiram about his drinking and subsequent behavior, Carlos expressed that he would quit drinking but that he would "make no promise, sign no pledge, and that he expected to take a drink occasionally."[141] With C.K.'s advancing age, the family grew more and more concerned about the terms of succession should C.K. die and leave the entire operation to Carlos as the present will stipulated.

Then, Carlos died suddenly on January 17, 1933, at the age of forty-one. The official cause of death was double influenza pneumonia, and he was said to have died at the home of friends in San Mateo. The illness, his obituary stated, developed rapidly and was "of the epidemic form that is prevalent in California." But Carlos's alcoholism was the real culprit. He had been to a Bay Area sanitarium at least twice and recovered briefly each time, Phebe recalled many years later, but he always relapsed. In

Carlos K. McClatchy Dies Of Pneumonia In San Mateo

Life's Work Ended

CARLOS K. McCLATCHY.

General Manager Of McClatchy Newspapers Ill Only Brief Time

Brilliant Career Of One Of West's Most Promising Young Journalists Closes In Untimely End

CARLOS KELLY McCLATCHY, vice president and general manager of the McClatchy Newspapers, editor of The Fresno Bee, and son of Charles K. and Ella K. McClatchy of Sacramento, died to-day of double influenza pneumonia at the home of friends in San Mateo.

Death came shortly before 10:30 o'clock A. M. while physicians worked vainly to save his life by means of oxygen, which kept him alive for several hours. He passed away peacefully shortly after his father and his wife arrived at his bedside.

ILLNESS DEVELOPED FAST.

The influenza pneumonia that proved fatal had a rapid outset, being of the epidemic form that is prevalent in California. Doctors explain this is either of the mild form and clears up quickly or is of rapid development with no hope.

Dr. Philip King Brown, chief of the medical staff of the Southern Pacific Hospital, with a corps of physicians, was in attendance. McClatchy's fever was mild at first but developed rapidly. He had been ill only a few days. Funeral arrangements have not been made.

Dynamic Newspaperman.

In the passing of Carlos McClatchy the West lost one of the most brilliant, progressive and dynamic of its newspaper personalities. Coming from a family of eminent California journalists—his grandfather, James McClatchy, founder of The Sacramento Bee, being a pioneer in the newspaper

zation of Sacramento Post No. 61, American Legion, and was chosen unanimously its first commander.

Due to his initiative in connection with legion activities, the veterans' organizations acquired the old City Library Building, in I Street, between Seventh and Eighth, which is now its headquar-

Carlos McClatchy's sudden death stunned family, friends and fellow journalists. The official cause of death was double influenza pneumonia, but his alcoholism was most likely the cause. *Photograph by Rebecca Crowther.*

counter to the official cause and place of death, Phebe said that he had been on what appeared to be a New Year's binge that resulted in his being soaked in a chilling rain. He was, again, checked into the sanitarium, but this time, he did not come out. He died in the sanitarium—not at the home of friends—with Phebe and C.K. at his side.[142]

Tributes poured into the offices of the *Bee*, including one from William Randolph Hearst noting that Carlos's death was "a loss to journalism" and from rival paper the *Sacramento Union*, which referred to him as "a power in journalism in this part of the state" and noted that he would be missed by "the press and public throughout the West."[143] Attesting to the personal nature of the McClatchy Company, employees from both the Fresno and Sacramento papers held all-night vigils with the body.[144]

While Hearst's sons were never successful working in the Hearst publishing empire, Carlos had proven himself extremely capable, hardworking and a man of vision where expanding the publications and entering broadcast radio were concerned.[145] Carlos had the McClatchy Company entrenched in radio long before Hearst could convince his newspapers to follow suit.

One is left to wonder, if Carlos had lived, whether he could have eventually advanced to a level that rivaled Hearst himself.

6

NEWS WARS, A NEW McCLATCHY IN CHARGE AND THE CALIFORNIA RADIO SYSTEM

Carlos always has seemed to me a typical example of six lines by, I think, Edward Rowland Sill:
At the punch bowl's brink,
Let the drinker think
What they say in Japan
First the man takes a drink;
Then the drink takes a drink;
Then the drink takes the man.
—C.K. McClatchy, 1932[146]

The sudden death of Carlos McClatchy changed everything for C.K. and the future of the McClatchy Company. C.K. had counted on Carlos continuing what C.K.'s father, James McClatchy, had started back in 1857. C.K. might not have realized that in addition to losing his son and the heir to the family media business, the McClatchy Company had lost perhaps its greatest innovator and visionary.

But with Carlos gone, the issue of "succession" was again up in the air. C.K.—aging, in poor health and so devastated at the loss of Carlos that he could not get out of the car at the graveside service—had to reconsider his will and the future of the company.[147] C.K.'s primary concern was that, upon his death, the McClatchy Company be overseen by a family member as president. A new agreement drawn up less than two months after Carlos died established Charles and Ella McClatchy as owners of all the common stock of the McClatchy Company with fifty thousand shares each and

C.K. and Ella McClatchy. C.K. was so devastated by his son's death that he could not get out of the car at the graveside service. *Center for Sacramento History*.

created a voting trust to secure future management of the corporation. The voting trust consisted of C.K. and Ella McClatchy, Eleanor McClatchy, *Bee* business manager G.C. Hamilton and J. Earl Langdon, the *Sacramento Bee*'s managing editor.[148] An addendum to C.K.'s will and the 1933 voting trust agreement directed that the trustees and board of directors elect his daughter Eleanor as president and director upon his death.[149]

While placing a woman in such a position of corporate power might appear to be forward-thinking in 1933, C.K.'s motives had nothing to do with a belief in Eleanor's ability to run the family business and everything to do with the business retaining a McClatchy at its head. In a supplemental statement attached to the 1936 addendum, C.K. specified that "the trustees both under the trust agreement and under my will shall be composed, in majority, of men," subject to a provision in his will regarding the appointment of his eldest daughter, Charlotte McClatchy Maloney.[150] C.K. also directed that any of his grandsons who showed an interest in learning the newspaper business, "including radio," be "given employment in whatever department of such newspaper or radio enterprises for which they show the most aptitude, and they should be advanced from time to time in unison with their abilities, capabilities and interest taken in their work." Overseeing the advancement of the grandsons, he noted, should be in the hands of general business director G.C. Hamilton and editorial director Walter P. Jones.[151] Eleanor was not mentioned in this addendum letter, nor were specifics of managing the radio enterprises, although the business of broadcasting and its relationship to the public airwaves was continuing to change.

The Communications Act of 1934

The Communications Act of 1934 was born out of the Radio Act of 1927, just as that act was the follow-up to the Radio Act of 1912. Each succeeding piece of legislation was required because something was left undone—or unsatisfactorily done—by the others. The FRC, created by the Radio Act of 1927, began applying the newly codified but not defined standard of the "public interest, convenience and necessity" when granting and renewing licenses and assigning frequencies. As we have seen, frequency shifts during this time created problems for smaller broadcasters, including the McClatchys.

As part of the new licensing process, the FRC established three categories of broadcast radio station, each with parameters for signal strength and service. These categories were clear channel (the high-powered stations that did not share their frequency assignment with another station), regional and local.[152] "General public interest" stations were commercial stations selling airtime to everyone and included not only the clear channel stations but most of the regional ones as well.[153] To the FRC, for-profit broadcasters fit the "general public service category" because the profit motive would induce these stations to provide programming desired by the market.[154] Stations classified as "propaganda" stations because they represented only one point of view were allowed to operate on low power and often shared frequencies. Hundreds of these small, nonprofit propaganda stations lost their licenses within three years of the passage of the Radio Act of 1927 due primarily to unfavorable time and frequency assignments mandated to them by the FRC. Very few license renewal applications were turned down by the FRC, yet by the fall of 1929 there were one hundred fewer stations on the air.[155]

In the 1930s, in the aftermath of signal reallocation, opposition emerged more strongly from nonprofit broadcasters and those individuals opposed to the increasing commercialization of broadcasting. This commercially supported system was referred to in the radio industry as the "American system of broadcasting," a term designed to distinguish the commercial nature of U.S. broadcasting from the state-supported model established in Great Britain. To be sure, labeling U.S. broadcasting the "American system" had public relations value. In an address before the Second National Conference on Educational Broadcasting, CBS president William Paley referred to the American system of broadcasting as a driving force for freedom, stating, "He who attacks the fundamentals of the American system attacks democracy itself."[156]

CBS and NBC had a tremendous stake in this American system. Within four years of the passage of the 1927 legislation, the two networks combined accounted for 30 percent of all U.S. radio stations, and all but three of the forty clear channel stations were owned by one of these two networks or their affiliates.[157] This type of commercial influence is what concerned radio reformers the most.

But the radio industry had leverage the reformers did not—NBC, CBS and the National Association of Broadcasters (NAB) in a sense controlled the airwaves that were becoming increasingly important to "publicly-conscious politicians." In addition, these same broadcasters had the knowledge and the wherewithal to undertake their own public relations campaign to promote the "innateness" of the "American system of broadcasting."[158] And while there was support for reform to be found in both houses of Congress, the leaders of relevant committees were almost unanimous in their support for the status quo where broadcasting was concerned.[159]

For his part, newly elected president Franklin D. Roosevelt chose not to take a position publicly on the broadcast debate, but in 1934, the president endorsed legislation to bring all communications regulations under a single administrative agency, an arrangement that pleased the commercial broadcasters. This legislation, which reinstated the Radio Act of 1927 and replaced the FRC with the Federal Communications Commission (FCC), was introduced in both houses with the intent of rushing it through committee hearings and bringing it to the floors of both the House and the Senate for a vote as quickly as possible. One of the reform groups, however, submitted an amendment to the bill while it was in committee hearings. The Paulist Fathers, headed by Father John Harney, proposed the amendment that would require the reserving of 25 percent of the channels for nonprofit broadcasters. The committee voted against this proposal, but Senators Robert Wagner of New York and Henry Hatfield of West Virginia agreed to introduce the amendment on the Senate floor.[160]

The Wagner-Hatfield amendment was the impetus for a flurry of public relations activity on both sides of the issue. The Paulists, who received the support of Catholic organizations and parishioners, were joined in the fight by organized labor. In response, the NAB geared up its lobbying efforts and attacked the amendment as an attempt to destroy "the whole structure of broadcasting in America."[161]

The amendment was defeated in both houses.

The Communications Act of 1934, signed by Roosevelt on June 18, was a victory for the commercial broadcasting interests and included every major point the NAB wanted. As one historian put it, although the legislation was signed by Roosevelt, the substance had Hoover "written all over it." Hoover had overseen the choices made at the outset of broadcasting and its regulation, and the Communications Act of 1934 served to ratify and consolidate those early decisions.[162]

The Communications Act of 1934 replaced the FRC with the FCC and vested the commission with authority to regulate all communications by wire and radio. It also reaffirmed the concept of the "public interest, convenience and necessity" as a key, although still largely undefined, component.[163] It was evident that "public interest" was not synonymous with "public access."

It was also evident that public interest was not synonymous with reporting the news.

The 1934 act did not include specific mention of news, but as news reporting became an increasingly important commodity for radio as well as print, an ongoing war for both advertising dollars and access to politicians and policymakers placed newspaper publishers and broadcasters in conflict. The conflict existed not only with radio stations but also with other newspaper publishers like McClatchy and Hearst, who had already broadened their media holdings to include radio stations as well as newspapers.

Commoditizing Information: The Press-Radio War

James C. Young, writing for *Radio Broadcast* in 1925, stated flatly, "The future of the press lies in the air." The prospect that most excited Young about a "newspaper of the air" is precisely what most worried newspaper publishers. Radio, even in its infancy, was becoming part of the "press" with the possibility that every thirty minutes, the most current news could be transmitted over radio rather than awaited in a daily edition of the local newspaper. As Young put it, "The man with a radio set may learn in the evening of some great event that his particular newspaper will not convey to him until the next morning."[164]

News over the radio seemed to be a natural fit, especially for those radio stations owned by companies like the McClatchy Company. The call letters for McClatchy stations KFBK and KMJ were used on the air only when legally necessary, with McClatchy preferring instead to refer as often as possible to the *Sacramento Bee* Station and the *Fresno Bee* Station, both on the air and in print, as a means of promoting the newspapers as their primary business.[165]

But most newspapers, especially smaller local papers, did not own radio stations. For them, broadcasting was a serious threat to their stock-in-trade—the gathering, writing and reporting of the news.

This conflict escalated into the "Press-Radio War."

Although the Press-Radio War has been largely viewed by media historians as the period from 1933 to 1935, when newspaper publishers and print journalists actively sought to control broadcasting's access to the news, the conflict extended for a much longer period of time and began with the earliest broadcasting of the news. Print journalists argued that radio news was a threat to society, due in part to the deviation of broadcast messages from the conventions of established newsgathering and dissemination. The argument was that, in some way, this different methodology violated moral, ethical and cultural standards, actually endangering the American public.[166] Print journalists had long been the gatekeepers of the news, the ones with access to newsmakers in positions of power, and the ones who standardized the language and delivery of the message. Radio threatened to shift the balance of power in newsgathering and distribution.

But this was not solely a case of protecting the interests of the public; economic issues were at the core of the dispute. Turf had to be protected, sources had to be jealously guarded, access had to be tightly controlled.

The American Newspaper Publishers Association (ANPA) complained that broadcasters simply helped themselves to news published in the newspapers and sold that "commodity" to advertisers. Once this practice became more widespread, newspapers sought to protect their property (the news they had gathered and written) from unauthorized broadcast by radio stations.[167]

Radio stations had not yet developed the staff and facilities for the regular gathering and reporting of the news. A 1928 published program schedule for KFBK did not indicate a news program for the station at all, nor did a schedule for 1930, although special public affairs programs such as President Hoover's speech before the American Bankers Association in

Cleveland, Ohio, were broadcast courtesy of KFBK's CBS affiliation.[168] It appears there was no "cross-pollination" between the reporting and editorial staffs of the *Sacramento Bee* and the station management and production staffs of KFBK.

In the late 1920s, sponsors were not interested in news programming because they did not perceive it had the audience interest that entertainment programming carried. But for broadcasters, news programs had two advantages: news could help build the station's hours of programming that could be considered public service and broadcasting the news was inexpensive from a production standpoint.[169]

The formation of NBC in 1926 and CBS in 1927 added to the animosity between the press and broadcasting as radio advertising began to increase and newspaper advertising began to decrease.[170] By the time the Depression hit, the battle lines were firmly drawn. National networks provided competition for advertisers, greater resources for investment in program production and a national audience, but at the end of the 1920s, what these networks did not have were formal news departments.[171] Interestingly, on December 1, 1928, KFBK's program schedule in the newspaper did not indicate a news program, as already noted, but did include the football scores, weather and a broadcast of the correct time—all elements of news but not news programming—in the limited 7:30 p.m. to 10:00 p.m. broadcast day. A display ad from San Francisco station KFRC running on the same page as the KFBK program schedule invited Sacramento listeners to tune in to KFRC at 10:00 p.m. when KFBK signed off to hear "Sacramento Night on KFRC," a program about the city and its citizens and featuring music and other entertainments "in honor of Sacramento" but no news.[172]

In 1928, the Associated Press (AP), United Press (UP) and International News Service (INS), as well as some local newspapers, agreed to provide the returns of the Smith-Hoover presidential election to radio stations as a public service. Their aim might have been an attempt to control the flow of information to radio stations by acting as gatekeeper of their news territory, but the result was a listening public that developed an interest in news as a regular feature of radio programming.[173] In December of that year, KFAB in Lincoln, Nebraska, introduced two daily news broadcasts and hired the city editor of the *Lincoln Star* to direct the programs. In 1930, KMPC of Beverly Hills, California, began airing a schedule of three fifteen-minute news shows daily and organized its own newsgathering service, the Radio News Service of America, with ten reporters covering the same beats as the Los Angeles newspapers and out-of-town correspondents under contract for other news.[174] A KFBK radio log for one week in September 1930 does not indicate any news programming whatsoever, nor does a published schedule for 1931. By 1932, however, KFBK was broadcasting a program called *Newspaper of the Air*. Presumably, the news being broadcast on KFBK came straight from the pages of the *Sacramento Bee*.

THE LITTLE EAGLET'S DISAPPEARANCE HAS THE NATION TUNING IN

In 1932, CBS, KFBK's national network affiliate, began broadcasting a sponsored news program presented by Boake Carter, an unknown radio announcer who would soon gain national prominence. At this time, the AP had adopted a policy that permitted radio stations to use news bulletins for stories considered to be of "transcendent importance," the perception being that radio could not possibly provide the kind of in-depth news coverage the public desired and that the public, upon hearing the news bulletin, would turn to the newspapers for the complete story.[175]

All that changed on March 1, 1932, with the kidnapping of the twenty-month-old son of aviator and national hero Charles Lindbergh—the "Lone Eagle"—and Anne Morrow Lindbergh.

The kidnapping of the Lindbergh baby fit within the definition of transcendent importance, and the AP and other wire services worked with radio stations to appeal to the kidnappers for the "Little Eaglet's" return. NBC, CBS and some local stations, presumably those in the general region of the Lindbergh's New Jersey home, sent their own reporters to cover the story. The result was the first national news story in which radio figured extensively, and this coverage by radio continued through the trial and conviction of accused kidnapper and murderer Bruno Hauptmann. Broadcasters like Boake Carter began attracting large audiences of new listeners for their broadcasts as they covered all the details of the tragedy.[176]

By 1933, the conflict between the press and radio had escalated. At their conventions, the AP's and the ANPA's radio committees recommended that press associations stop supplying news bulletins to radio stations in advance of newspaper publication, and that bulletins supplied for broadcasting be no more than thirty words in length and not be available for advertising sponsorship.[177]

In response, CBS organized the Columbia News Service. Utilizing foreign reports from Exchange Telegraph and Central News in England, other foreign newsgathering agencies and "stringer" reporters in various U.S. cities, CBS established a competing news service and signed on General Mills as a national sponsor. In retaliation, newspapers in a number of cities pulled all listings of CBS programs from their papers.[178]

The *Sacramento Bee*, however, did not pull CBS program listings. At this time, KFBK was affiliated with CBS and the Don Lee Broadcasting System. Radio schedules published in the *Bee* included both CBS programs and the Columbia News Service airing on the station.[179]

The move by CBS to aggressively pursue its own network news strategy was regarded as a very real threat by the ANPA. When CBS filed an application with the National Press Club in Washington, D.C., requesting that its reporters be admitted to the Congressional Press Galleries, the application was denied on the grounds that gallery admission was

View of the beautiful KFBK studios at 708 I Street. The radio station adjoined the *Sacramento Bee* building on Seventh Street.

reserved only for those representing "daily newspapers or newspaper associations." CBS challenged this ruling, taking the complaint to the Senate Rules Committee to seek an amendment to the existing gallery rules, but the strong opposition from print journalists and publishers resulted in a denial of the appeal.[180] In this case, "press" related more closely to "printing press" than to the media in general.

By this time, CBS and NBC (which had also established a news department but on a much smaller scale than CBS's) were amenable to some form of agreement with the ANPA. In December 1933, representatives of NBC, CBS, AP, UP, INS and the NAB met with the executive committee of the ANPA's Publishers' National Radio Committee (PNRC) and drew up the ten-point "Biltmore Agreement."[181] The provisions of the agreement were announced to all newspaper publishers in a January 5, 1934 letter. One of the main provisions of the agreement was the formation of the Press-Radio Bureau (PRB), a news agency that would supply reports to radio.[182]

Assuring compliance proved to be impossible. Independent radio stations refused to conform to the agreement and instead formed their own radio services or used the services of newly formed competing bureaus. For the West Coast, opposition to the Press-Radio Bureau included the added issue of a lack of West Coast coverage. In addition, the Western Union and Postal Telegraph wire transmission fees required to receive the reports were too high. In response, the PRB established a West Coast bureau in March 1934.[183]

As the Press-Radio Bureau plan began to break down KFBK began making other news arrangements of its own. The *Sacramento Bee* inaugurated its first crossover of editorial staff to the radio station side in 1935 with *Bee* sports editor Rudy Hickey, who began a program series called the *KFBK Sports Parade*. By 1936, the KFBK-published schedule specified "the latest news reports furnished by the *Sacramento Bee*."[184]

The PRB had lost much of its effectiveness. Broadcasters were dissatisfied with the service, "outlaw" bureaus like the Transradio Press provided a perhaps "unfair" level of competition and UP and the Hearst-owned INS removed themselves from the Biltmore Agreement so they would be free to compete head to head with Transradio. The PRB limped along until December 1938, when a final withdrawal of financial support from CBS and NBC killed it.[185]

THE CALIFORNIA RADIO SYSTEM: McCLATCHY AND WILLIAM RANDOLPH HEARST STRIKE A DEAL

On June 18, 1935, as the Press-Radio War was nearing its end, the FCC granted permission for KFBK to increase power from one hundred watts, where it had been since the beginning, to five thousand watts. The Sacramento station was also granted permission to operate on a twenty-four-hour broadcast schedule.[186] Still the only radio station in Sacramento at this time, the increase in both power and length of broadcast day positioned KFBK for even further expansion as a regional multimedia company.

In addition to the power boost, KFBK changed network affiliation to NBC. Sacramentans received program offerings from both the NBC Red and NBC Blue networks. On January 11, 1936, KFBK began broadcasting from new studios utilizing a new transmitter station.[187] Other changes came to the McClatchy Company as well. C.K. died in April 1936, and his daughter Eleanor—per the legal provision put in place upon Carlos's death—took over as president.[188]

Almost immediately, Eleanor McClatchy showed her commitment to continuing her late brother's goal of making the McClatchy Company a large, far-reaching multimedia firm by completing a project he had started.

On November 21, 1936, McClatchy Broadcasting Company, the new entity formed on March 14 of that year as a wholly owned subsidiary of the McClatchy Company, entered into a partnership with Hearst Radio Inc. and the Evening Herald Publishing Company, both belonging to William Randolph Hearst, to form the California Radio System (CRS).[189] The initial structure of the network involved six stations, each station able to sustain its national network affiliation but also receiving local-, regional- and state-specific programming as part of the CRS. The original stations in the network were KEHE in Los Angeles, owned by the Evening Herald Publishing Company; KYA in San Francisco, owned by Hearst Radio Inc.; and KFBK in Sacramento, KERN in Bakersfield, KMJ in Fresno and KWG in Stockton, all owned by the McClatchy Broadcasting Company.[190]

"Much credit for the rapid expansion of the McClatchy Broadcasting Company," a *Bee* article noted, "was due to the foresight of the late Carlos K. McClatchy, editor of *The Fresno Bee* and organizer of the radio system."[191] The article was subtle, but it stands to reason that without Carlos's business savvy and foresight in establishing McClatchy radio stations at key points up and down the state of California and without his network of contacts and the reputation he had developed, Eleanor could not have put the California Radio System together during her brief and sudden appearance at the head of the family business.

But in November 1937, Hearst withdrew from the partnership. At this time, Hearst's interests were being divested by a trustee in a virtual bankruptcy.[192] When Hearst withdrew, McClatchy Broadcasting Company retained sole control of the network, operating it as one of its departments through 1943. Hearst station KYA remained with the network under a contract of affiliation. The other Hearst station, KEHE, was replaced by KFWB in Hollywood, the Warner Brothers station, which also supplied a new series of programs featuring "the finest talent of the world's motion picture capital" for broadcast on the CRS. The network also added McClatchy station KOH in Reno and stations KFOX in Long Beach and KTMS in Santa Barbara.[193]

In 1936, the McClatchy Broadcasting Company and Hearst Radio launched the California Radio System, a statewide regional radio network. *Photograph by Rebecca Crowther.*

The announcement of the changeover to complete McClatchy control and the addition of the Warner Brothers station was a sudden one. Hearst Radio's relinquishing of all interest in the statewide network was announced in the *Bee* on Saturday, November 6, 1937, with McClatchy assuming complete control on Monday, November 8. Offices were maintained in both San Francisco and Los Angeles, but the operation's headquarters was established in Sacramento. All McClatchy stations were part of both the CRS and NBC.[194] Initially, the enterprise proved to be a profitable one, garnering almost $110,000 net profit after agency commissions in 1938.[195]

In the same newspaper article, McClatchy also announced that the FCC had granted another authorization to increase signal strength. McClatchy Broadcasting Company, which now referred to itself as a pioneer in western radio, was scheduled to boost power for KFBK from five thousand watts to ten thousand on December 15, 1937, giving it the most broadcasting power in the CRS chain. KFWB in Hollywood and KYA in San Francisco remained at five thousand watts, KMJ in Fresno at one thousand watts and KWG in Stockton and KERN in Bakersfield at only one hundred watts of power.[196]

7

ELEANOR McCLATCHY: THRUST INTO THE SPOTLIGHT AND HIT WITH NEW CHALLENGES

As the boys grow up I want you and the other trustees to pick out the one the most available and the best armed to direct the course of the paper, because I think a man ought ultimately to be in charge.
—C.K. McClatchy, 1936

During World War I when Carlos was in the army and away from Sacramento, other men in uniform made their way to California's capital city. One of those handsome young officers was Raymond L. Crozier of Pasadena, California. According to Phebe, Raymond and Eleanor became friends and then decided to marry. Because Raymond was not Catholic, the wedding took place in the back garden of C.K. and Ella McClatchy's home rather than in the church; Phebe McClatchy served as matron of honor. The newlyweds moved to Pasadena. The marriage, however, was short-lived and lasted only about four years.[197]

"Raymond was involved in some business affairs, I don't know what the business was," Phebe recalled. "They [the McClatchys] thought he imposed on her and tried to get her money and evidently she thought so too, because she was unhappy and wanted out." It was Carlos who made the arrangements for Eleanor's divorce from Raymond. She had written to her brother that she wanted to leave the marriage, and Carlos took care of the details. After the divorce, Eleanor returned home to Sacramento. In 1928, she had the marriage annulled by the Catholic Church on the grounds of nonconsummation.[198] Eleanor's interest was not in marriage, the family media enterprises or her ex-husband's business ventures. Her

Eleanor McClatchy married Raymond L. Crozier in the garden of her parents' home. The marriage was annulled within a few years. *Center for Sacramento History.*

interest lay in the theater, and after her annulment, that interest took her to New York.

When C.K. needed Carlos to help with the *Bee* just after his son graduated from Columbia, the directive to come home was given and heeded. Now, with Carlos gone and the future of the business of growing concern to C.K., again the directive was given for a child to come home, and the command was, once again, heeded. C.K.'s request made it plain that Eleanor was to enter the family business, listen, learn and be a placeholder until a suitable male McClatchy was deemed ready to take the helm. As C.K. wrote to her in February 1936:

> *Now I may last for years and I may not last a year. Everybody connected with us thinks you ought to come into* The Bee *and learn the various propositions—not to interfere, but to have a knowledge of everything that is going on when I pass away, so that in after years when the time comes for*

> *you, you may be thoroughly equipped to manage matters. I think everybody connected with* The Bee *looks favorably upon this proposition. Of course you understand that some years necessarily will have to pass before you can pass from an observer to a real director. As the boys* [Carlos's sons, James, Charles Kenny and Ellery] *grow up I want you and the other trustees to pick out the one the most available and the best armed to direct the course of the paper, because I think a man ought ultimately to be in charge.*[199]

If Eleanor McClatchy never intended to enter the newspaper business, certainly no one else intended for her to, either.

When Carlos was pleading his case before C.K. to take on a more independent role in the McClatchy enterprise, he pointed out in his argument to his father that his sisters, Eleanor and Charlotte, benefited from the business revenues but contributed nothing.

Eleanor, who had planned to be a playwright and not the head of a large media company, left New York in February 1936 at her father's request and returned to Sacramento to learn the business of the *Bee* and its holdings.

But C.K. died a mere two months after Eleanor's return. Although Eleanor had no "on the ground" experience in running the multimedia enterprise, she had grown up around the business, understood her father's business philosophy and had the valuable resources of an excellent staff in place upon which to draw.[200]

Although Eleanor seems to have shared Carlos's vision of a multimedia business, her approach was decidedly different from what her brother's had been. It was also during this period, from the mid-1930s into the post–World War II era, when information—the news—became as much a commodity as the entertainment aired on radio. And entertainment, in the form of broadcast radio programs, was increasingly and more openly identified with and sponsored by advertisers, both national and local. Eleanor's soon-to-be-realized vision of the airwaves as public service and her interpretation of what constituted the public interest would shape media in California's capital region and significantly impact the profitability of broadcasting for the business—and not always in a positive direction.

The McClatchy Broadcasting Company continued to pursue a reach that exceeded its grasp during this time and, in the process, brought greater media innovation and entertainment offerings to the people of the Sacramento region, many presented commercial free. It also brought technical advances that combined both the newspaper and broadcasting sides of the family's media holdings.

RADIO FACSIMILE AND THE NEWSPAPER OF THE AIR

What if your daily edition of the *Sacramento Bee* or the *Fresno Bee* could be ready and waiting for you inside your home when you awoke? It's an intriguing idea for the 1930s—and one that brought the newspaper and broadcasting sides of the McClatchy media enterprise together.

In October 1937, the McClatchy Broadcasting Company applied to the FCC for a special experimental license that allowed the Sacramento-based media firm to use a new technology, radio facsimile, to broadcast a newspaper directly into homes in Sacramento and Fresno. As with radio, the Sacramento company was the first on the Pacific coast to incorporate the new technology into its media business.[201] The newspaper, called the *Radio Bee*, was written and transmitted in the KFBK studios, with Fresno affiliate KMJ receiving the transmission by wire from Sacramento. The initial distribution reached a mere one hundred participants due to a lack of available receiving equipment at the time. McClatchy reportedly invested between $30,000 and $50,000 in an RCA transmitter and one hundred receivers for the experiment. The receivers were placed in fifty homes each in Sacramento and Fresno to be rotated every three weeks to new area residents selected by an impartial committee.[202] The *Radio Bee* was in a two-column format; eight pages in length (size eight and a half by eleven); contained news stories, photos and comics; and was transmitted into homes with receiving sets in the early morning hours.[203] The RCA receivers installed in the one hundred test homes operated by means of a radio signal that activated a high-speed printer bar, which pressed down on a spiral steel wire rotating at a rate of seventy-five revolutions per second. Printing paper and carbon paper were passed around a cylinder

The McClatchy Broadcasting Company's pioneering use of facsimile technology garnered recognition by *Business Week* as the first instance of network facsimile broadcasting. *Center for Sacramento History.*

Fresno Fair Edition **THE RADIO BEE** Fresno Fair Edition

Vol. 1 Fresno, September, 1938 No. 2

NEW MARVEL ON DISPLAY

New Medium Is Pioneering Step In Radio History

Fresno: The introduction of facsimile by the McClatchy Broadcasting Company marks another pioneering step in the history of McClatchy Newspapers, owners of the Fresno Bee, the Sacramento Bee and the Modesto Bee.

Years ago, while other newspaper publishers were looking for means of combatting the growth of radio, which they saw as a threat to their existence, McClatchy Newspapers decided to acquire radio stations and get into this new field themselves. They were among the first newspapers in the entire nation to own radio stations and today their group of five stations is one of the largest independently owned groups in the United States.

Now with facsimile making its bow, it is the McClatchy Broadcasting Company which pioneers in the West this new medium of dissemination of the news.

Facsimile Seen As Television Forerunner

Fresno: Facsimile, which is being demonstrated for the first time in Central California at the Fresno District Fair utilizes some of the basic principles of television.

Engineers in charge of the facsimile experiments point out that facsimile prints the image mechanically while television flashes the image by means of electron beams upon a glass screen.

Facsimile Exhibit Brought To Fresno Fair By Bee Radio Station KMJ

Visitors to the Fresno District Fair are among the few people in the United States who have had the opportunity to witness facsimile, the sensational new newspaper by radio, in operation.

Shown at the California State Fair in Sacramento for the first time on the Pacific Coast, the facsimile exhibit was brought to Fresno by the Fresno Bee radio station KMJ in order to give their listeners a first hand view of the new radio marvel.

The introduction of facsimile marks another progressive step in the history of radio, heralding the not far distant time when printed reports of the news of the day will be delivered to your home by radio.

Many Fair Exhibits Show Valley Wealth

Fairgrounds: The tremendous wealth of Fresno County and its neighboring counties of the San Joaquin Valley is amply demonstrated by the numerous agricultural exhibits to be seen on the grounds of the Fresno District Fair.

Although long known as the center of California's grape industry, few people realize that Fresno County is also among the leading producers of many other agricultural products.

Enlarged Racing Program Attractive

Fairgrounds: Increased interest in the racing events at the Fresno District Fair is expected by Fair officials as a result of their efforts to bring to the racing strip some of the finest performers on the California Fair circuit.

Many famous names among California breeders have sent their horses to Fresno for the events here. An increase in the pari-mutuel handle will probably be one of the most noticeable results.

KMJ Will Start Facsimile Newscasts

Fresno: KMJ will soon begin regular facsimile news broadcasts using the same frequency now used for radio broadcasting, 580 kilocycles.

The Federal Communications Commission in Washington, D. C., has granted the McClatchy Broadcasting Company a special experimental license to conduct field tests of facsimile broadcasting in Central California. Early this Fall the actual broadcasting will begin with KMJ transmitting facsimile from 12 midnight until 6 A. M. Receivers will be placed in more than two score homes within a radius of fifty miles from Fresno.

RADIO BEE MARKET PAGE

S. F. Livestock

SOUTH SAN FRANCISCO, (United States Department of Agriculture)—No early sales, asking strong to higher or above 9.50 on good to choice 170-225 lb. butchers; some interests talking around steady, undertone strong.

Cattle, 600. Steers and medium to good she stock in light supply, few early sales today; load good steers from local feed lot 8.25 averaged 912 lbs.; heifers very scarce; short load good range cows 5.50; medium grades 5.00@5.25; fat dairy type cows, 4.50@4.75; bulls steady, medium grades eligible to 6.00.

Calves, 50. About steady; odd head good to choice vealers 9.00@9.50, truck lot medium 220 lb. weights 7.50 straight.

Cash Grain

CHICAGO, Sept. 13.—(AP)—Cash wheat No. 3 red 67½; No. 4 hard 64½; No. 5 63.

Corn: No. 1 mixed 53½@54½, No. 3 53½, No. 1 yellow 54¼@55, No. 2 53½@55, No. 1 white 54¾, No. 2 54¼.

Oats: No. 2 mixed 25, No. 3 25½, No. 2 white 27@28, No. 3 24¾@26¾, sample grade 23.

Barley actual sales No. 3 47@62 No. 4 56, sample grade 31@47, range 31@66 nominal, clover seed red top 7.00@7.75 nominal, timothy seed 2.75@2.80 nominal buckwheat 2.10@2.25 nominal.

Flax

MINNEAPOLIS, Sept. 13.—(AP) Close: September 1.68, December 1.68½.

Dow Jones Averages

(Final)—Furnished by Dean Witter & Company. Thirty industrials 137.06 off 4.84, twenty railroads 27.48 off 1.23, twenty utilities 19.13 off .76, forty bonds 88.87 off .40.

Butter And Eggs

SAN FRANCISCO, Sept. [illegible]3.—(Federal State Market News and Grading Service).

Large standards [illegible]½c
No. 2 candled, medium [illegible]½c
No. 1 small [illegible]½c

Local Quotations

Quotations on eggs to the retail trade here issued by the Poultry Producers of Central California are as follows:

Large extras 35c
Large standards 31c
Medium extras 32c
Small extras 20c

Petaluma quotations: Large 31c; medium, 27c; standards, unquoted; small, 16c; checks, 13c.

Butter

(Fresno prices paid to retail dealers are 2c to 4c higher).

92 score, 27½c; 91 score 26c; 90 score, 25½c; 89 score, 2[illegible]c.

Eastern Fruit Prices

Below we list prices realized today on California fruits in the East. The following is submitted by the California Fruit Exchange:

New York

Pears—Box Bartletts 1.50@2.30.
Grapes—Lug Thompson Seedless 90c@1.60, lug Ribiers .45@2.15, lug Red Malagas 1.10@1.25.
Figs—Box Calimyrna 80c@1.30, box Kadotas 80c@1.30, box Black Missions 55c@75c.

Chicago

Pears—Box Bartletts 1.55@1.90.
Grapes—Lug Thompson Seedless 1.30@1.35, lug Red Malagas 1.20, lug Ribiers 1.85, lug White Malagas 1.00.
Plums—Crate Giants 95c@1.10, crate Presidents 85c@1.05, crate Grand Dukes 80c.

London Bar Metal

LONDON, Sept. 13.—(AP)—Bar gold 142s 8½d, up ½ penny. (Equivalent $34.77).

Bar silver 19 3-16d, off ⅛. (Equivalent 42.06 cents).

Chicago Grain

CHICAGO, Sept. 13.—(AP)—Wheat prices backed down more than a cent a bushel today under the pressure of profit taking and stop loss selling.

Weakness in securities influenced selling here. Increased European political tension, credited with being an important factor in the stock market, fell flat in the wheat pit. Normally war talk is an influence for higher grain prices.

Wheat closed ⅝ to ⅛ lower compared with Saturday's finish, September 63⅞@64; December 65½@65⅝; corn was ⅜ to ¼ down, September 52½@52⅝, December 51¼; oats unchanged to ⅜ lower.

Metal Market

NEW YORK, Sept. 13.—(AP)—Copper steady; electrolytic spot 10.12½; export 10.12. Tin easy; spot and nearby 42.80; forward 42.90. Lead steady; spot, New York 4.90@4.95; East St. Louis 4.75. Zinc steady; East St. Louis spot and forward 4.75. Pig iron, No. 2, f.o.b. eastern Pennsylvania 21.00; Buffalo 20.00; Alabama 16.00. Aluminum, virgin 99 per cent 20.00. Antimony, spot 14.00. Quicksilver 76.00@80.00. Platinum, pure 39.00. Chinese wolframite, duty paid 18.00@20.00. Nominal.

Wool Tops

NEW YORK, Sept. 13.—(AP)—Trade buying met a scarcity of contracts in wool top futures trading today and early easiness was overcome. Markets abroad closed weak. Roubaix values declined 100 to 130 centimes and Antwerp was off ⅜ to ⅝d.

Hops

NEW YORK, Sept. 13.—(AP)—Hops steady; Pacific Coast 1937s, 15@17; 1936s, 12@14.

While the original *Radio Bee* was a two-column format, this special edition for the Fresno Fair is set in three columns. *Center for Sacramento History.*

where the printer bar impulses from the radio signal caused the spiral wire to press the carbon and printing paper together to form each segment of the words and images. As each line in the transmission registered on the paper, the cylinder moved into position for the next line.[204]

Appropriately, considering the *Bee*'s forward-looking stance concerning the medium of radio, the first *Radio Bee* was transmitted on February 2, 1939, the seventeenth anniversary of the *Bee*'s inaugural radio broadcast on KVQ. The *Bee* was the first newspaper west of the Rocky Mountains to engage this technology and only the fourth newspaper in the country to do so. *Business Week* reported the Sacramento inaugural broadcast to be "the first instance of network facsimile broadcasting."[205]

The object, of course, was expansion of the business. Innovation potentially means new customers, new markets and, ideally, new sources of revenue. It is likely no accident that one of the first demonstrations of the technology was at the 1939 Pacific Coast Division convention of the American Association of Advertising Agencies. Once the technology became viable on a much larger scale, penetration into a new market, such as subscribers receiving the *Bee* newspapers by radio facsimile, would have opened up a new avenue for advertising revenue and advertising agency involvement.

Comics were also part of the *Radio Bee*. This Fresno Fair edition shows a full two pages of comics. *Center for Sacramento History*.

For some industry watchers, this technology was seen as another potential intrusion into the territory of newspapers. As one article noted, "One of the most obvious uses of facsimile is to supply news, news pictures and illustrative material. The availability of frequency modulation (FM) for transmitting facsimile opens a new field of development, free from practical limitations on the number of frequencies available, and with the added advantage of combination with sound frequency modulation broadcasting."[206]

McClatchy Broadcasting saw this technology as a means of reaching families in rural areas, giving them the services of a metropolitan newspaper "on a par with their urban friends." A newspaper printed in their homes while they slept would be an alternative to day-old news arriving in the form of the printed newspaper under a more traditional delivery method.[207]

Unfortunately, as often happens with technology on the forefront, the return on investment did not exceed the state of the art at that time. The experiment into radio facsimile proved to be both expensive and too slow. Although the McClatchy Broadcasting Company dropped the project in 1940,[208] it continued to focus on expansion, innovation and new markets as the media landscape so long dominated by McClatchy was changing.

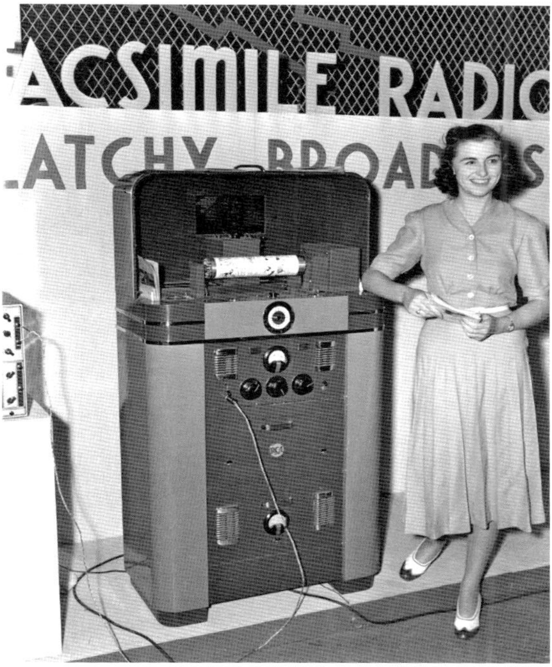

Left: A young woman demonstrates the RCA transmitter for facsimile radio.

Below: The facsimile transmitter on the left and the receiver that would have been in the home on the right. *Center for Sacramento History*.

Boxing champion Max Baer Sr. clowns around in the KFBK studios, circa 1951. *Center for Sacramento History.*

By 1939, Sacramento residents were supporting two radio stations. Local car dealer Royal Miller received a license from the FCC in 1937 to broadcast with one hundred watts of power. The McClatchy Broadcasting Company, begun in 1936 and maintaining an extensive engineering department to support its own stations, lent the services of its engineers to build Miller's newly licensed KROY (the ROY chosen as short for "Royal"), helping to usher in the small station that initially broadcast from the Sacramento Hotel at Eleventh and K Streets.[209] While this move to aid a direct competitor seems unusual, it was neither the first nor the last time a McClatchy enterprise made a move of this sort. Another Sacramento radio station, KCRA, licensed in 1945, would also benefit from the expertise of the McClatchy Broadcasting Company Engineering Department. A similar move had been made by C.K. McClatchy in 1929 when he loaned William Dodge, a newspaperman from Southern California, $350,000 to buy rival Sacramento daily the *Union*, keeping that morning paper alive. However, it has been suggested that, although C.K.'s exact motive is unknown, the move to keep the *Union* in business might have been an attempt at keeping a stronger competitor out of the Sacramento market.[210]

Even in the midst of the Depression, radio was profitable thanks to advertising. Advertising-supported programs brought a great deal of popular entertainment into people's homes courtesy of NBC and CBS. But control of the sources of advertising revenue, especially on a national scale, attracted the attention of the recently created FCC, which expressed concerns about monopolistic practices as would-be competitors failed to successfully rival the two national networks.

BROADCASTING CHAINS AND THE FCC

In December 1938, the *Congressional Digest* published its "Pro & Con Monthly" under the topic "Is There a Monopoly in American Radio?" The issue included a recounting of how broadcast radio operates, the origin of American radio laws and an explanation of the investigation by the FCC of the radio industry. Threat of monopoly was the primary concern. The charge that an independent had no chance to enter into competition with the established chains was at the core of the investigation. Representatives of the chains asserted there was no monopoly, as evidenced by the competition among NBC, CBS and the Mutual Broadcasting System (MBS) to produce and broadcast the best programming. The fact that the listening public was able to decide where they wanted to tune their radio dials was the result of that competition. Contributors on both sides of the debate included David Sarnoff of RCA and NBC, William Paley of CBS, members of Congress, an FCC commissioner, a member of the National Association of Broadcasters (NAB) and others.[211]

To understand what led to the investigation, one must understand the business and operational structure of the chains. What were then called "chains" later became known as "networks," the term that persists in common usage today. I use the terms "chain" and "network" interchangeably here. Chains began as an experimental process in the years just prior to the formation of NBC in 1926 and the formation of CBS in 1927, making these two entities the broadcasting chains on the "ground floor" of this new business enterprise. The purpose of the chain was to link stations together so those stations could simultaneously share identical programming.[212]

Concerns about the business practices of chains arose in the late 1930s as it became apparent that entering the network business was virtually impossible for an outsider. The outsider in question was a consortium of four powerful radio stations—WGN of Chicago, Cincinnati's WLW, Detroit's WXYZ and WOR in Newark. For these four stations, the move to form a chain made sense. Much of the quality programming they offered listeners was produced in their own studios, and they realized if they worked together they could reduce costs for each of them.[213] Their endeavor, Mutual Broadcasting System (MBS), began with a 1934 stock issue and consisted of those four stations and no affiliates. The founding four had been at one time affiliated with either CBS or NBC but left due to compensation issues. Rather than follow the already established network model of owning affiliate stations, MBS was owned by its foundation stations and functioned more as a "program exchange and syndication service."[214] MBS began with the four owner stations, but others soon joined, attracted by the better compensation scale. MBS paid stations the full station rate card fee for broadcast time less a 5 percent commission and expenses. The compensation structure was better than that of the established networks, and the programming was some of the best locally produced programming in the country.[215]

The other thing MBS did was make statements to the FCC and other government agencies about the near impossibility of a new competitor getting established in commercial radio. The reason for the difficulty was the affiliate structure of the other networks. Stations that were in large, desirable markets or had a license that allowed high-powered transmission were already bound by contractual agreement as affiliates to either NBC or CBS. In 1936, NBC's contract with affiliates bound the station to the network for five years, although NBC had the option to terminate a contract after one year if the network desired. CBS had a similar contractual agreement in place. The result was a system in which the two major networks controlled most of the advertising revenue. From 1935 to 1937 NBC, which had two networks, known as the Red and the Blue, garnered 29 percent of the broadcast advertising volume, CBS had 20 percent and MBS had less than 2 percent. Local and regional advertising made up the remainder.[216]

Concerns over monopolistic practices went beyond the chains themselves, however. In addition to the contractual lock up of the most desirable affiliates, NBC and CBS also had an arrangement with AT&T whereby the two networks paid less for their use of the transmission lines. When AT&T ultimately reduced its landline rates, the company that saw the greatest direct benefit was MBS.[217]

The FCC's inquiry into the business practices of chain broadcasting began in 1938. When the hearings got underway, the first to speak before the commission was RCA president and NBC chairman of the board David Sarnoff.

When it came to radio broadcasting, the concern over unfair business practices went beyond the question of public interest to include access to affiliates and advertising revenue and whether or not there was real competition for those advertising dollars. In his remarks before the FCC, Sarnoff declared:

> *The American people have a free radio because they have a broadcasting industry that pays its own way. Those who object to commercial announcements on the air are apt to forget that it is the revenue from*

> *these announcements which makes it possible for them to hear regularly a symphony orchestra conducted by Toscanini, the broadcasts of the Metropolitan Opera, America's Town Meeting of the Air, the National Farm and Home Hour, the Damrosch Music Appreciation Hour and many other costly sustaining features of the networks.*[218]

In Sarnoff's description, competition in network broadcasting was a competition for both the listener's attention and the advertising dollar. Ownership of any particular network, he noted, did not determine competition. "If there are no listeners there are no advertising dollars, and if there is no service there are no listeners." If there are two networks and no variety, listeners, he maintained, would seek options elsewhere.[219] In other words, audience preference would ensure competition and a place for competing networks.

The FCC's *Report on Chain Broadcasting*, released in 1941, acknowledged the value and quality of the programs produced by the networks and that those program offerings to the American people were made possible in large part by advertising revenue brought to the radio industry through the "network method of broadcasting to Nation-wide audiences." Simply stated, the bigger audiences brought in advertisers and revenue that paid for quality programs. Chain broadcasting, the FCC acknowledged, "plays an essential part in the development of the broadcast industry. But the fact that the chain broadcasting method brings benefits and advantages to both the listening public and to broadcast station licensees does not mean that the prevailing practices and policies of the networks and their outlets are sound in all respects, or that they should not be altered."[220]

This set the tone of the report. The FCC acknowledged the role advertising played in providing free programs of quality to a national audience—the "public" whose interest, convenience and necessity is codified in radio legislation—but made it clear that network policy, where business structures and practices were concerned, could be separated from other segments of chain broadcasting and restructured if necessary. By the FCC's own admission they were not solving "all questions of public interest with respect to the network system of program distribution."[221] The FCC concluded their goal was to ensure the maintenance of a competitive market:

> *Radio broadcasting is a competitive industry. The Congress has so declared it in the Communications Act of 1934, and has required the fullest measure of competition possible within physical limitations. If the industry*

> *cannot go forward on a competitive basis, if the substantial restraints upon competition which we seek to eliminate are indispensable to the industry, then we must frankly concede that broadcasting is not properly a competitive industry. If this be the case, we recommend that the Congress should amend the Communications Act to authorize and direct regulations appropriate to a noncompetitive industry with adequate safeguards to protect listeners, advertisers and consumers. We believe, however, that competition, given a fair test, will best protect the public interest. That is the American system.*[222]

Sarnoff and NBC had a great deal about which to be concerned. At the time, NBC's two networks, the Red and the Blue, had licensed or affiliated stations located in a swath from New England to Omaha, Nebraska, and north of the Mason-Dixon line, covering only one-third of the United States by area but with a broadcasting "lock" on two-thirds of the country by population.[223] One of the primary concerns that came out in the FCC report was the means by which NBC and CBS exerted control over the broadcast operations of their affiliates. As the FCC pointed out, "It is the station, not the network, which is licensed to serve the public interest." The licensee is responsible for determining which programs air on the station. An affiliate station could not be bound by network contract into accepting *all* network programs. "The licensee is obliged to reserve to himself the final decisions as to what programs will best serve the public interest."[224]

In an appendix to the *Report on Chain Broadcasting*, the FCC included a list of regulations targeting the responsibilities of the licensee and limiting the network's power over its affiliates. The regulations included FCC refusal to grant a license to a standard broadcast station having a network arrangement that did not allow the station to broadcast programs from other networks or that had a network contractual agreement of longer than one year. The license refusal also disallowed network control of affiliate broadcast airtime or station rates. Taking direct aim at NBC, licensees were not allowed to affiliate with a network organization that maintained more than one network.[225]

When the FCC published its findings the McClatchy Broadcasting Company contacted the NBC Blue network, with which it had affiliated KFBK in 1939, and immediately made changes to the existing network contract. As part of the contract modifications, NBC Blue would, at its own expense, extend program transmission lines to the control board of the main studios of KFBK and offer the McClatchy station the first option to broadcast all NBC Blue programs scheduled to be broadcast in

Sacramento.[226] The FCC had concluded that network practices limited the licensee's freedom to choose the programs best suited to the public interest of the community, yet only the licensee had that responsibility.[227] As soon as the FCC proceedings concluded, the McClatchy Broadcasting Company wasted no time in exercising that newfound freedom.

Mutual Broadcasting System put forth its own assessment of the commission's findings. In his first white paper, released after the 1941 report, MBS general manager Fred Weber responded to what he called the alarms sounded by NBC, CBS and the NAB in the wake of the May 3, 1941 release of the report. This report did not, he assured his readers, abolish network broadcasting, did not do away with the American system of broadcasting, would not bring chaos, would not "paralyze the freedom of the air," did not threaten the continuation of network programming service and would not lead to government ownership of radio.[228] Pulling no punches, MBS reiterated key facts brought out in the report: NBC and CBS operated three national networks "controlling eighty-five percent of the nation's nighttime power," the net income from the operations of these two companies regularly "equaled about one-half that of the entire broadcasting industry" and the other half was "thinly spread" among the almost eight hundred independently owned stations, many of which operated at a loss. By operating two networks, MBS pointed out, NBC had been able to block competition by making rate concessions to advertisers that were not available to a single-network company.[229]

Weber released a second white paper that October in which he analyzed the FCC revisions. The white paper stated that the commission's order and amendments had "inaugurated an era of fair and equal competition so that in the future the success of a network will depend not on artificial restraints and unreasonable control over station independence but on its ability to furnish superior service to its affiliate stations, to the public and to the advertiser."[230]

The FCC's findings published in the *Report on Chain Broadcasting* resulted in the divestiture of one of NBC's networks. In 1943, NBC Blue was sold to Edward Noble, owner of New York station WMCA, and in 1945, it became the American Broadcasting Company (ABC). The FCC regulations regarding chain broadcasting did not, however, impact the regional chains like California networks CRS and Don Lee.[231]

With newspaper ownership of radio—as well as the structure of regional networks—untouched by the FCC findings, the McClatchy Broadcasting Company continued its integration of print and broadcast media. The broadcast side of the McClatchy enterprise held an estimated combined worth of $400,000 for the California radio stations, approximately five times their original purchase price. This growth in station value translated to increased listenership as the number of households with radios continued to grow, making the medium still more attractive to advertisers.[232] Key for McClatchy was what had always been its most saleable commodity—the news. Just as the *Sacramento Bee* had long been a source of local, regional and national news, McClatchy Broadcasting would offer the same level of advertising-supported news service to the listening public.

In 1939, largely in response to the Roosevelt administration's close attention to any conservative political leanings by sponsored news commentators on the major networks, both NBC and CBS issued guidelines for news reporting. The guidelines stated reporting was to be based in fairness, fact and without the personal opinions of the radio broadcaster, additional commentary or "microphone manner designed to cast doubt, suspicion, sarcasm, ridicule or anything of that sort" on the news as it is presented.[233]

The McClatchy Broadcasting Company published its own in-house set of rules and procedures to be followed in preparing and airing a radio news

Above and opposite: The lobby and the studios of KFBK at 708 I Street, circa 1948. *Center for Sacramento History*.

broadcast. It included instructions for preparing wire service copy and other written news for radio, reminders about maintaining local contacts and news sources, fact-checking all information before air time and a focus throughout on the importance of the news to the listener:

> *There has been too much tendency by radio to ignore local news and report only the national, foreign and regional news as carried by the wire services. Newspapers—and particularly the McClatchy newspapers—do a thorough job of local and regional news coverage. If people are interested in* reading *this news, they certainly are interested in* hearing *it...KFBK and KMJ occupy enviable radio positions in regard to local and regional news coverage by having available the output of the* Bees. *The stations and papers should cooperate as closely as possible in all news respects, with the stations plugging the papers on all possible occasions, and the papers calling attention to the station special events and featured newscasts.*[234]

McClatchy Broadcasting Company instructed its radio station news departments that commercial announcements must not total more than three minutes of a fifteen-minute news show aired during the day and not more than two and a half minutes of a fifteen-minute news program aired at night. The news broadcast would have no opening commercial with the exception of sponsor identification and perhaps a slogan or short product description. Long commercials at the start of the news, it was noted, would drive listeners to other stations. The news programming was to always air at the same time during the broadcast day, "day in and day out, year in and year out, so listeners will know automatically when to turn to them."[235]

It seems odd today to think of having to point this out. From a marketing standpoint, this sort of consistency and reliability builds listener loyalty. Listener loyalty creates a regular audience, and a consistent audience is what is sold to advertisers.

MASS CONSUMPTION, CONSUMER PRODUCTS AND ADVERTISING

> *I like to broadcast for OLD GOLDS. You see those OLD GOLD folks don't ask me to tell you that OLD GOLD is the only good cigarette. They concede that there are other good smokes. So the net of my radio talk is this: Try a pack of OLD GOLDS and "Let Your Taste Decide!"*[236]

Popular CBS radio announcer David Ross appeared in an Old Gold cigarette newspaper advertisement in the *Sacramento Bee* on the page that also listed the radio programming schedule. A final tagline in the ad reminded *Bee* readers to "TUNE IN on Fred Waring and his Pennsylvanians every Wednesday night—Columbia Chain," the show on which Ross appeared.[237] The Columbia Chain, CBS, was the network with which KFBK was affiliated at that time, and Fred Waring was a nationally popular musician and bandleader. This sort of cross-marketing tie is indicative of just how profitable McClatchy's newspaper-owned radio business model could be. Because KFBK was a CBS affiliate, the station received compensation for the broadcast hours in which network programs like the Old Gold–sponsored *Fred Waring and His Pennsylvanians* aired. Old Gold, capitalizing on its sponsorship of the national program, used the radio show's popularity to promote its cigarettes in newspapers whose readership had the opportunity of tuning into the radio program. The *Sacramento Bee* received ad revenue from Old Gold for the newspaper ad as well as compensation from CBS for the Old Gold show's airtime. Placement of the ad on the radio page of the *Bee* served also to call the

Host Frank Allen brought his show *Market Basket* to the Broderick Market. Image circa 1949. *Center for Sacramento History*.

reader's attention to the fact that KFBK was the CBS affiliate and that this was where listeners should tune their radios to hear the David Ross/ Fred Waring program. Although KFBK was still the only broadcast radio station in Sacramento at this time, listeners in the greater Sacramento area had the option of tuning in to San Francisco area stations like KGO and KFRC rather than listen to their local station.

The Old Gold newspaper advertisement and corresponding radio program were similar to marketing plans followed by other companies. Using radio advertising to make the listener conscious of, in this case, a cigarette's brand identity—and by extension, its desirability—increased sales. Other methods were also employed. Station contests that encouraged listeners to submit entries were used as a means of gauging audience numbers and identifying the regions from which the radio station drew. By engaging the listener, this method also served to ingrain brand identity. A 1930 coffee word contest aired by J.A. Folger & Co. over KFBK netted a report of 491 contest responses and showed the station, as well as advertisers, that the listening audience came from a much larger territory than previously thought. Although KFBK's business manager did not feel he could claim the entire territory as receiving consistent radio reception, he reported contest entries from Chico, ninety miles away; Oroville, seventy-five miles away; and Stockton, Yuba City, Marysville and Placerville, all fifty miles away.[238]

In 1928, the American Tobacco Company undertook a marketing experiment that illustrated the success of radio, branding and the impact of both on a consumer's need to buy a particular product. Helen Woodward, a former advertising copywriter and account executive, wrote, "The most desperate copywriters in the advertising business are those who have to write about cigarettes. What can they say? Tests have shown that hardly anyone can distinguish one brand of cigarette from another."[239] And yet a decade before Woodward wrote her article for the *Nation*, George Washington Hill of American Tobacco proved there did not have to be a difference in order to get the consumer to select a particular brand. American Tobacco sponsored the "Lucky Strike Dance Orchestra," a program Hill created. The show debuted on thirty-nine NBC stations in September 1928. To test the effectiveness of radio as an advertising medium, Hill pulled all other Lucky Strike advertising for a period of time, and in November and December, Lucky Strike sales increased by 47 percent. Radio alone had driven consumers' brand selection. Hill's success was soon emulated by Camel cigarettes and other product advertisers.[240]

In general, the Depression decade reversed the advertising spending level of the 1920s as the overall volume of advertising dropped. Yet the number of radio stations expanded and the listener base grew. Radio was thriving.[241] An article in a 1932 issue of *Business Week* pointed out that as other industries suffered, radio was profiting:

> *It is like going into a different world when you leave the depression-ridden streets for the office of a big broadcasting company. Men going past are fat and cheerful. Cigars point ceilingward, heels click on tiles, the merry quip and the untroubled laugh ring high and clear. In a corner office a vice-president broke down and confessed: "Sure, we're making money. Has it got to the point where that is a crime?"*[242]

The Depression-era vision of abundance promoted by President Roosevelt placed a new emphasis on spending and consumption. Advertising became both an economic force for price regulation and a vision of how the American culture worked, with product, advertisement and medium blended together into a representation of the culture itself.[243]

Other Depression-era advertisers on KFBK included local car dealer Capitol Chevrolet, Safeway Stores, Sears Roebuck & Co. and Dean Witter & Co. *Sacramento Bee* radio listings included the programs on Bay Area stations KGO, KPO, KSFO and KFRC, so *Bee* readers would have a full radio schedule; however, only KFBK's program sponsors were listed in the newspaper alongside the programs they sponsored.[244] A KFBK advertiser,

Inside the KFBK studios at 708 I Street. *Right*: Barbara Fankhauser, campus reporter; *left*: a young woman reads a script on air, possibly for Weinstock-Lubin Department Store. Image circa 1948. *Center for Sacramento History.*

whether local, regional or national, received additional market exposure in the pages of the *Bee*.

What impact did advertising on KFBK have on local patterns of consumption during the 1930s and 1940s? It is difficult to tell. At this time, factors such as the "media mix" of an advertising campaign—that is, a combination of media such as newspaper combined with radio combined with billboards—make any one medium's effectiveness difficult to track without specifically surveying customers as to what brought them into the store or how they learned about the product. Radio was, however, becoming an increasingly important part of people's daily lives. In 1936, more than three million Americans were enjoying the experience of "motor tours" accompanied by a car radio; in fact, manufacturers were anticipating a huge market for automobile radios in 1937. As one industry watcher noted, "The radio seems destined to be the most popular item of extra equipment on the models for the next year. They are coming fully prepared for the installation of sets."[245] The audience for radio continued to grow, and now it was mobile. Advertising increased with the growth of the audience numbers.

By the end of the 1940s, Sacramento's advertisers and consumers supported four radio stations: KFBK 1530 broadcasting at 50,000 watts, KROY 1240 at 250 watts, KCRA 1320 at 1,000 watts and KXOA 1470 at 1,000 watts.[246]

There was new competition in Sacramento's media marketplace, and a new look for both McClatchy radio and newspapers. In 1943, as the United States was involved in World War II, Eleanor McClatchy approached Walt Disney with the proposal that he create two caricature representations—twin bees. The famous illustrator, who had created popular culture icons Mickey Mouse and Donald Duck, agreed to the proposition as long as his earnings for the project were donated, in some way, to the war effort. Scoopy, the newspaper-wielding bee, is still in use today. Gaby, the bee at the microphone, was the symbol for McClatchy radio for the remainder of its existence. A third bee character—Teevy, created by a Disney staff artist—would be added later for

At Eleanor's request, Walt Disney drew twin bees for the McClatchy Company. Scoopy, left, is still in use today. Gaby, holding the KFBK microphone, represented the broadcasting side of the company. *Center for Sacramento History*.

This 1944 group photograph and cartoon caricature of the "25 Year Club" labels Eleanor McClatchy, shown holding Walt Disney–drawn bee Scoopy, as the "Boss." *Center for Sacramento History*.

the company's television stations. Creating Scoopy and Gaby cost $1,500, all of which was sent to the Army Relief Fund per Walt Disney's instructions.[247]

Under Eleanor's direction, the McClatchy companies supported the war effort in a variety of ways, some extravagant and public, others very private and almost anonymous, as Eleanor herself preferred to be. The newspapers endorsed scrap metal and rubber drives, collecting books for servicemen, the planting of victory gardens and other supportive activities on the homefront. The *Fresno Bee* staff swung into action in a more direct way. They collected photographs of Fresno-area babies born after their fathers had shipped out, packaged the photos along with weekly summaries of community news and mailed them to "local boys" overseas. Eleanor, who maintained her interest in the theater, organized a theatrical troupe that toured California military bases. The troupe performed a show called *Naughty Naught* and raised about

The KFBK Players in 1944. Eleanor never gave up her theatrical roots, and she sent performers to military bases during World War II. *Center for Sacramento History.*

$5,500 from civilian audiences. The money was then donated to finance entertainment facilities on military posts. As a more personal gesture, Eleanor—Miss McClatchy as she was known in the offices of the *Bee* for the remainder of her life—sent cartons of cigarettes as holiday gifts to *Bee* employees stationed overseas.[248]

Radio station programming also reflected a commitment to the war effort. Special broadcasts over KFBK included such features as the dedication of the new Camp Kohler Signal Corps Training Center near Sacramento and a report by a representative "Navy Mother," Mrs. Irene Schafer of Glendale, recently returned from the Great Lakes Naval Training Station. The navy mother reported on the health and happiness of all navy mothers' sons during the "Meet Your Navy" program.[249] Programs like *At Your Service* acquainted Sacramentans with war work being done in their community, special broadcasts of programs like *What's Doin' Ladies?* were turned over to war bond drives and all of the 1945 home and road games of Pacific Coast

The Sacramento Solons in their 1947 home opener at Edmonds Field. American servicemen who were part of the Army of Occupation in Japan reported hearing the rebroadcasts of Solons games. *Center for Sacramento History*.

League baseball team the Sacramento Solons were broadcast locally without commercial sponsorship, and then rebroadcast at 3:00 a.m. for the benefit of troops in the Pacific. After the war, American servicemen stationed with the Army of Occupation in Japan reported hearing the broadcasts of the games quite clearly.[250] It was more than entertainment; it was a taste of home sent over the airwaves.

8

POSTWAR ECONOMIC BOOM AND THE ENTRY INTO TELEVISION

The air waves belong to the people, not to private business.
—Eleanor McClatchy, 1969

In the 1940s, Charles Hull Wolfe of Batten, Barton, Durstine & Osborn Inc., later known as advertising giant BBDO, conducted a survey of the impact of radio as measured by consumer recall of advertised products. His survey focused on nationally advertised packaged products: coffee, dry cereal, gelatin dessert and household soap products. Two hundred middle-income homemakers in New York City were asked where they had seen or heard ads for various products. Radio ads received the highest results for all products except coffee: 84.3 percent for household soap products, 75.0 percent for gelatin dessert and 88.6 percent for dry cereal.[251]

Another study, undertaken by H.D. Wolfe of Kent University's Bureau of Business Research, looked at the factors influencing the buying habits of women who did not work outside the home. Interviews were conducted with 1,256 middle-income homemakers in urban and rural areas of Ohio. It was found that radio influenced more purchases of specific items than any other medium—10 to 35 percent of product sales were attributed to radio.[252] An additional survey by Wolfe of 205 druggists and grocers in New York City showed that 92.1 percent of druggists found radio best for selling their products, and 89.8 percent cited radio as the type of national advertising their customers talked about when buying branded items. Of grocers, 87.3 percent felt radio was best for selling their products, and 88.9 percent of their customers named radio in relation to brand items.[253]

Local stations were also reaping the benefits of the effectiveness of advertising on radio. A study that focused on local and regional businesses advertising on radio consistently throughout 1942 showed that of 794 local firms interviewed for the study, only 6 indicated that radio advertising was unsuccessful. This local advertising was mostly "spot" advertising rather than sponsorship of an advertiser-produced show as was common with national advertisers.[254] By 1936, spot radio achieved new growth as national advertisers sought to buy non-network radio time on local and regional stations. While the network sales grew by 10 percent, spot radio sales grew by 64 percent.[255]

The McClatchy Broadcasting Company prospered during this time in each of its local markets. The preliminary "Analysis of Station Broadcast Revenues" report submitted to the FCC for 1945 indicated that after paying all agency commissions, KFBK revenues for selling station airtime to a network, national and regional sponsors or local advertisers was $285,845. KMJ in Fresno cleared $351,560, KERN in Bakersfield earned $96,229, KWG in Stockton was at $82,790 and KOH in Reno netted $100,468.[256] As California entered the postwar era, McClatchy's profits were set to grow as consumption was encouraged nationally as the means to economically convert from a wartime to a peacetime economy, and personal wants (no longer needs) could be fulfilled while one engaged in the "civic duty" of consuming.[257]

But Eleanor McClatchy's vision of radio had taken a distinct turn from the commercial model that had brought the stations to the 1936 value level reported in the McClatchy Broadcasting application to incorporate.

The postwar era was an economic boom for the Sacramento region. Between 1945 and 1950, Sacramento County grew at a rate faster than the state of California. In the early years of the postwar era, Sacramento County's population growth increased 62.7 percent compared with the state's overall increase of 53.3 percent. Much of the growth during the war years was tied to the expansion of civilian employment at military posts and the railroads in the region. In addition to this civilian labor force, Sacramento County also saw an influx of the families of military servicemen. The Sacramento region continued to grow after the war thanks to what was perceived as strong prospects for continued economic expansion.[258] The bulk of this population growth was due to a large volume of migration from other states. The attraction was straightforward: California residents had higher than average per capita incomes and buying power, the climate was mild and the existing growth encouraged

The KFBK FM tower (left) and the 708 I Street studios with the FM tower in place, circa 1947. *Center for Sacramento History.*

still more growth. "Growth begets growth, and fast-growing California has always looked like a land of opportunity to the young and hopeful east of the Rockies," one economic survey pointed out.[259]

Among the key industries in this region were three military installations: the Army Signal Depot, which functioned as a large army supply and repair center for military communications equipment; McClellan Air Force Base, one of the largest air force supply and maintenance bases in the United States; and Mather Air Force Base, which served as a training site. Local, state and federal government, as well as manufacturing, provided much of the employment opportunities for Sacramentans. By 1955, McClellan and Mather Air Force Bases and the Army Signal Depot were the largest employers in the area, and their employees had significant buying power in the region.[260] Buying power translated into consumption, and as real estate developers moved housing options farther away from the central city, shopping changed as well. One of Sacramento's earliest shopping centers, Town & Country Village, opened in 1946, and other suburban shopping centers and the region's first mall followed in short order.[261]

Broadcaster Enid Day, the producer and presenter of a successful radio program for a Florida retailer, put her knowledge of the power of radio as key to retail success into print in 1947. *Radio Broadcasting for Retailers* reminded retailers that the point of a radio program was to catch the attention of the listener. "If you are able to catch and hold the ear of your radio audience the law of averages will turn some of them into customers."[262] This, essentially, is how all sponsored radio programs worked. A loyal listener, one who enjoys a program enough that they will tune in with regularity, is very likely at some point to be converted from a sales prospect to a customer.

Sacramento department store Weinstock-Lubin knew this. Not only did it have a program airing on KFBK, but it also provided the ideal venue for live broadcasts by the McClatchy station—the corner show windows of its Twelfth and K Streets store. When the Pacific Coast League Sacramento Solons baseball team was on the road, KFBK sportscaster Tony Koester took up residence in the Weinstock-Lubin corner window to broadcast the game. Reading the action off a ticker tape, Koester added his own sound effects to create the "feel" of being at the ballgame. These broadcasts drew large crowds to the department store to listen and watch Koester in action. It is almost certain that many of these fans did some shopping in the store as well.[263]

Converting prospects into customers on a mass scale was made even easier with the growth of consumer credit and borrowing. Nationally, total

KFBK sports broadcaster Tony Koester brought listeners Sacramento Solons "away" games from the corner window of Weinstock-Lubin Department Store at Twelfth and K Streets. *Center for Sacramento History*.

consumer credit grew more than ten times between 1945 and 1960, and installment credit, fueled primarily by car purchases, increased nineteen times during the period.[264] The growth of credit cards in the postwar era contributed a great deal to increased consumption. Cold war–era propaganda equating the mass consumption of goods and the creation of prosperity as the "American way of life" (versus an image of a Soviet system in which the free choice of the consumer did not exist), bolstered the new American ethic of consumption and the immediate fulfillment of desires through new products.[265]

It is unclear exactly when Sacramentans began using credit cards, but area consumers had been accustomed to buying on the installment plan since the 1920s, when credit terms were used as a means to encourage automobile purchases.[266] Sacramentans, just like their counterparts in the rest of the country, were able to begin amassing greater levels of consumer debt.[267] As KFBK celebrated its increase to fifty thousand watts of power in 1948 with a special section in the *Sacramento Bee*, the interconnectedness of the newspaper, the radio station, consumer spending and the local businesses that used both media to reach their customers became obvious. One of the largest advertisements in the newspaper section was for Maleville Bros. Electrical Appliances, located in the recently opened suburban Town & Country Village shopping center at the corner of Fulton and Marconi Avenues. The ad prominently featured the logo of the shopping center as well as the logo of the business. The primary focus of the ad was a General Electric Radio-Phonograph Cabinet priced at $315 and available on credit terms. The ad shows off the beautiful, large mahogany cabinet that featured both AM and the newer FM bands—the McClatchy Broadcasting Company had launched KFBK-FM in 1947—and storage space for 120 records.[268] This created something of a consumer feedback loop. The newspaper section featured an ad for a business promoting its shopping center location, selling a high-end version of a common product on credit terms, giving the consumer a lovely piece of furniture for his or her new suburban home and encouraging the family to listen to the radio station featured in the newspaper section in which the ad appeared.

But the celebratory KFBK special section revealed something more than the radio station as a vehicle to advertisers. In addition to touting KFBK's technical pioneering in radio facsimile and paying homage to the *Sacramento Bee*'s own radio pioneer Carlos McClatchy, the multipage newspaper section showed that the McClatchy Broadcasting Company was very aware of its role in serving the public interest. Special programs included a neighborhood

Construction of the fifty-thousand-watt antenna and the new KFBK transmitter control room, 1948. *Center for Sacramento History.*

preview of the transmitter for residents of Pleasant Grove, where the new transmitter was located, station visits to seven communities in the Sacramento County region and the Sacramento origination of an ABC network audience participation show, *Surprise Package*, featuring national emcee Jay Stewart.[269] Most significantly, though, was the article concerning KFBK's schedule of farm programming. Noting that "daily activities on thousands of farms in the Sacramento Valley are geared to the news and information received through agricultural programs over KFBK," the article went on to describe two daily farm broadcasts at 6:45 a.m. and 12:45 p.m.—broadcast times that were selected based on the farm work schedule. In addition to the daily programs, the weekly *McClatchy Farm Review* airing Saturdays from 6:30 to 7:00 a.m. on the six stations of the McClatchy Broadcasting Company boasted the expertise of a special radio station news department that included a full-time farm editor and an agricultural staff. "The agricultural service program is presented in the public interest. With a finger on the agricultural pulse of the nation, the farm editor gives a concise interpretation of the top farm news of the day, from the nation's capital, the state capital, the fairs and farm centers, the University of California, the College of Agriculture in Davis, Yolo County…the 4-H clubs, the Future Farmer Chapters and all the way points on the main line of agriculture,"[270] the article noted. This type of extensive public service programming could only come from a radio station with a predominantly local and regional focus. National broadcasting and entertainment-oriented regional chains would not find a positive return on investment for this type of programming. According to one chronicler of the McClatchy business holdings, the programming was not profitable for the McClatchy stations either, but Eleanor insisted that agricultural and 4-H programs continue in a strictly public service capacity. Under her edict, farm programming was to contain no advertising whatsoever.[271]

From the beginning, Eleanor McClatchy believed radio should be more of a public service than a commercial enterprise. For her, public service equated to public interest.

One of her most unique public service radio projects was *La Escuela Espanola del Aire de KFBK*, a 1941 program consisting of fifty-four lessons in Spanish. The course was broadcast each morning and then again in the afternoon for those who wished to review the material. It was designed to teach beginners Spanish by hearing and repeating. The program, according to one source, was the first of its kind in the country, and listener/pupils from California, Montana, Colorado, Utah, Idaho,

Residents of Pleasant Grove were invited to tour the new transmitter control room as KFBK prepared to go to fifty thousand watts in 1948. *Center for Sacramento History*.

Nevada, Oregon and Washington took advantage of the radio language lessons. Letters received at KFBK told of listening classes that had formed to take advantage of the lessons in a group setting. Unfortunately, the program was discontinued when the United States entered World War II.[272]

In 1944, Eleanor—again harkening back to her theater roots—established the country's first "little theater of radio" on KFBK, eventually expanding it to other McClatchy Broadcasting stations. The goal of the program was to develop local volunteer talent for the production of radio plays.[273] In speaking to a group of McClatchy Broadcasting employees in 1969, decades after her vision of commercial-free public service programs had begun airing, she reiterated her view that "the air waves belong to the people, not to private business."[274]

Nationally, radio broadcasting and its advertising revenues were going through a significant change. By 1949, advertisers were cutting their radio advertising budgets and commitments in order to make the shift to television, this in spite of the fact that the cost per thousand (CPM)

Agriculture programs were one of several types of programming Eleanor McClatchy determined should be aired commercial free. Image circa 1947. *Center for Sacramento History.*

viewers reached by television was considerably higher to advertisers than the CPM for radio. The expense of television production, combined with the fact that there were far fewer televisions in homes than radios at this time, made television advertising a less effective and more costly advertising approach than radio. Nationally, radio listening was at 98.2 percent versus 1.8 percent for television, and radio "sets-in-use" continued to increase between 1947 and 1948.[275]

As radio was changing nationally, locally owned media in Sacramento was changing regionally. KFBK-FM made its first broadcast on February 22, 1947—exactly twenty-five years after KVQ's inaugural broadcast made the McClatchy Company a multimedia pioneer. Between 1948 and 1956, Eleanor McClatchy added six FM stations in Reno, Nevada, and California's Central Valley, including KERN-FM in Bakersfield and KBEE in Modesto.[276] At Eleanor's insistence, and in keeping with her view of public service programs serving the public interest, the FM stations emphasized commercial-free agricultural news, educational programs, classical music and cultural offerings. While this appealed to Eleanor's theatrical side and her desire to "bring culture to the masses," it also proved to be unprofitable.[277]

In a 1956 letter to Eleanor, her nephew James—Carlos's son—expressed his concerns:

> *The thing we must recognize is that apparently as long as we run the radio stations as we do, they are going to lose money. This does not discount all the modifications and adjustments that already have been made in an effort to keep the lid on losses. If those things had not been done, the losses would have been much greater.*
>
> *The next point is that if we decide as a matter of policy to operate at a loss, the losses logically cannot be questioned.*
>
> *But if it has not been decided to do that as a matter of policy, then logic requires one to consider a program for eliminating the losses.*
>
> *And I cannot avoid the conclusion that something must be done about the radio losses.*
>
> *Our firm is not rich enough to continue absorbing them. We have too many other current and future major expenses. Since the losses are made up from newspaper profits it constitutes an unfair drain upon the newspaper resources.*[278]

Of course, the radio stations *had* been profitable at one time, back when James McClatchy's father, Carlos, was working with them. James

Carlos McClatchy's sons, Charles Kenny (C.K.) McClatchy (opposite) and James Briggs McClatchy (above). *Center for Sacramento History*.

reminded Eleanor of that in his letter. "I suppose," he wrote to his aunt, "the basic question is whether or not the radios—in the face of changed operating conditions—ever are going to support themselves again."[279]

The "Little" Station with the Big Signal

The assertion in 1931 by *Sacramento Bee* business manager G.C. Hamilton that the McClatchy Company did not believe in "high-powered stations" continued through the 1940s in principle, if not in fact.[280] A succinct definition of "high-powered stations" had been posed by Senator C.C. Dill, one of the key figures in crafting the Radio Act of 1927. In a December

1928 newspaper article carried in the *Sacramento Bee*, he referred to high-powered stations as those broadcasting with fifty thousand watts of power and whose signal dominated radio receiving sets within a radius of 150 to 200 miles. Dill was a proponent of limiting radio broadcasting stations to ten thousand watts of power except for experimental purposes. Although Hamilton, speaking for the *Sacramento Bee* and therefore speaking with the voice, at that time, of C.K. McClatchy, commented that the *Bee* did not believe in such power, it is hard to accept that Carlos McClatchy—with his vision that often ran counter to the tight rein held by his father—would not have jumped at the chance to broadcast with fifty thousand watts as a high-powered station back in 1931.

While McClatchy Broadcasting Company's 1948 celebration of KFBK's increase to fifty thousand watts put the pioneering local station in the high-powered category fifteen years after the death of visionary Carlos McClatchy, the attitude of the station regarding its local and regional mission, due in large part to Eleanor's vision of what radio should be, remained on the "small station" level. The emphasis was on treating the definition of "public interest" as though it referred to a local constituency, not a generalized national standard. The fact that KFBK retained a full-time farm editor and the McClatchy Broadcasting Company had an agricultural staff, operating as though the radio station served the public in the same manner as a newspaper, was indicative of local radio attempting to meet what was felt to be the needs of its local public—the listening audience. In a region that boasted three of the West's largest fruit- and vegetable-processing plants, a national soup manufacturer (Campbell's) and the largest almond-processing plant and rice mill in the United States, providing agricultural service programs in addition to entertainment *did* serve the public interest. So did the language program, performance opportunities, commercial-free broadcasts of the local baseball team and baby pictures sent to servicemen overseas.[281] But those programs could have been sponsor vehicles as well, and there would have been no lack of sponsors lined up to spend their advertising dollars to reach those audiences. Had the radio stations been profitable, some of that cash could have been leveraged for further media expansion.

Television was on the McClatchy radar, and entry into television was a move that Eleanor wholeheartedly endorsed. But although the McClatchy Broadcasting Company applied to the FCC in 1948 to operate a television station, it would be many years before a Sacramento license was granted. In fact, it was 1952 before the FCC even managed to *look* at the McClatchy applications for Sacramento and Fresno stations.[282]

KOVR-TV on Arden Way in Sacramento, circa 1983. *Center for Sacramento History.*

Fresno proved to be no problem. That permit went through uncontested, and on September 18, 1952, McClatchy Broadcasting was granted a permit for UHF channel 24. KMJ-TV went on the air on May 31, 1953. The Fresno television operation was housed in the old radio station offices at the *Fresno Bee* building for six years until a permanent studio was built.[283]

Sacramento was a much more difficult proposition. McClatchy Broadcasting's application for Channel 10 was contested by a group calling itself the Sacramento Telecasters Inc. Although an FCC examiner—after a series of hearings—recommended granting the license to McClatchy in 1953, the FCC body disagreed. Sacramento Telecasters won the license on the grounds of diversifying control of the mass media. It was the first time the FCC had ruled in a licensing dispute based solely on the fact that one of the parties concerned had other media interests. The FCC's decision was contested, but a District of Columbia appeals court upheld the FCC's decision on the license. McClatchy Broadcasting appealed to the U.S. Supreme Court, but the court chose not to hear the case. Further appeals proved unsuccessful, and the company gave up on Channel 10 in February 1958.[284]

On April 1, 1965, McClatchy Broadcasting finally had its Sacramento television station. George Williams welcomed the viewing audience with these words: "This evening McClatchy Broadcasting presents to you its new TV station, KOVR, Stockton-Sacramento…offering you in the next two hours a sampling of the kind of local programs in store for you on Channel 13." It had been forty-three years since Sacramento's first radio broadcast on the short-lived but pioneering KVQ, and now, McClatchy Broadcasting reached back to that touch point to launch television:

> *It was the night of February 22, 1922…a night to remember…this little man George Plunkett adjusted the cat's whisker on his crystal set and tuned in…he heard…*
> *(whang-whang! Buzz-buzz!)*
> *…a voice! (buzz-buzz! Bang!)*
> *…music!*
>
> *George and 599 other crystal set owners…600 in all…were listening to the first broadcast of voice and music over KVQ, a phenomenal little giant of 5 watts…that broadcast thereafter for two hours nightly!*
>
> *In 1922 it was indeed a phenomenon for KVQ was one of five broadcasting stations in the whole western United States! And the first newspaper owned station west of the Rockies. It was owned by the* Sacramento Bee.
>
> *Here is the control room of KVQ. It's* [sic] *tiny 5 watts had an uncanny way of throwing its strength around the country in such a fashion that after only 10 months broadcasting, it was politely invited to go off the air by the Federal Broadcasting authorities. It seems its signal became so wild that it was said to interfere with stations as far East as Buffalo, N.Y. Ah, well! Poor, brave pioneering little KVQ. At least it had helped lead the way to a whole new world of broadcasting on the Pacific Coast.*[285]

Although Eleanor's goal of adding television to the broadcasting arm of the company was realized in 1964 with the purchase of KOVR, eventually the company divested itself of all broadcasting and returned strictly to the business of newspapers. It is interesting to speculate how things might have been different if Carlos had lived to take over the McClatchy Company and McClatchy Broadcasting upon C.K.'s death in 1936. Carlos McClatchy brought an intense business focus to the family enterprise, combined with a bent toward innovation; one wonders just how far he could have taken the broadcast side of the McClatchy Company. Eleanor

Charlie Duncan played Cap'n Delta on a popular KOVR cartoon show. The draft sketch of the advertisement shows cartoons that aired, including the Beatles, Yogi Bear, Mr. Magoo and Woody Woodpecker. Image circa 1965. *Center for Sacramento History.*

McClatchy brought her love of art to her new position and made it her mission to make education and culture widely available. Her father never had the time to groom her for the role, yet she knew and strongly held to the principles and practices of her father. Where Carlos was a journalist from an early age and highly focused on growing the McClatchy media holdings and seeking out new opportunities, Eleanor had grown up "around" the business but not "in" the business. While her focus on cultural offerings available to all was admirable and certainly fulfilled a need, her insistence on turning down advertising for some programs she deemed to be of a public service nature likely hurt the broadcasting properties in the long run. Perhaps it can be said the foray into broadcasting by the McClatchy Company proved that radio broadcasting could not serve the public (or the public interest, however it might be defined) without, as the reformers wanted, an entirely new system of broadcasting—a system that allowed for commercially viable general entertainment along with support for "not-for-profit" educational and public service programs.

As with Eleanor McClatchy's vision, reform would have required a financial means of supporting programming that *serves* the public rather than *sells* to it. Of course, then the questions become who decides what the public needs to hear? Who is the arbiter of culture and good taste?

Who determines what fills the "ether" when you tune your radio?

9

PUBLIC INTEREST, PUBLIC SERVICE AND A PROMISE KEPT TO C.K.

U.S. Supreme Court justice Potter Stewart once famously declared that he may not be able to define pornography, but "I know it when I see it."[286]

The concept of the public interest as applied to broadcasting likely first came from Secretary of Commerce Herbert Hoover in a speech before the Fourth Annual Radio Conference in 1925. His statement—"The ether is a public medium and its use must be for a public benefit"—did not define the concept, but the attendees at the conference endorsed it in principle and recommended it be incorporated into legislation they all agreed was needed to tame the chaos of the ether.[287] As can be seen through the Radio Act of 1927, the Communications Act of 1934 and the influence of networks and for-profit commercial broadcasters on how American radio was structured and who was allowed to have a voice on the air, unlike pornography, Congress, the FRC and the FCC did not know the public interest when they saw it.

Congressman Wallace H. White Jr., one of the key figures in drafting the legislation that became the Radio Act of 1927, acknowledged that a definition of "public interest" could not be agreed upon by the conference delegates, but that there had to be some criteria for limiting the number of broadcasting stations. Operating for the benefit of the public became a key way to exercise the necessary control. "If enacted into law," White said of the need for legislation agreed upon at the conference, "the broadcasting privilege will not be a right of selfishness. It will rest upon

Both Carlos and Eleanor McClatchy felt strongly about serving the public interest; they just approached that service in decidedly different ways. *Center for Sacramento History*.

assurance of public interest to be served."[288] Both Carlos and Eleanor took this to heart; they just interpreted it in different ways.

Between the end of World War I and the passage of the Radio Act of 1927, the business of radio broadcasting in the United States developed rapidly. When Congress passed the Radio Act of 1927 as a means of regulating broadcasting, it did so without an understanding of either the realities of the new medium or its potential. The "ether" was in a state of chaos with more stations operating than could be accommodated by the limited wavelengths in the broadcast spectrum. Legal challenges to the power given to the secretary of commerce to assign wavelengths as well as issue licenses resulted in many stations broadcasting on whatever channels they chose. The resulting signal interference caused a great deal of frustration among the listening public. The Radio Act of 1927 was the result of legislation introduced in both houses of Congress with the intent of settling the means by which broadcast licenses and signals were allocated. Use of the airwaves was a conditional, not an absolute, right and one to be accorded to a broadcaster only if the licensed station served the public interest, convenience and necessity.[289] That phrase—"public interest, convenience and necessity"—was borrowed from public utility legislation and was never clearly defined in regard to broadcasting. The Radio Act created the Federal Radio Commission (FRC) and vested the commission with broad regulatory powers driven primarily by this public interest standard. For independent, local radio stations like the *Sacramento Bee*'s KVQ and then KFBK, the rapidly changing regulatory

Eleanor never lost her love of the theater and remained a strong supporter of the performing arts in Sacramento. The Eleanor McClatchy Performing Arts Center bore her name. *Center for Sacramento History.*

landscape of broadcast radio at the hands of Congress and the FRC had an immediate impact on station operations not felt by larger stations and networks with the clout and contacts to influence regulatory policy.

Without a definition of "public interest" it is unclear whose interests held prominence in the eyes of the FRC as regulation developed and stations like KFBK in Sacramento flexed to adapt to those ill-defined standards. But the story of the McClatchys and their work in broadcasting shows what happens when a committed station owner puts their version of "the public interest" at the forefront of the business model.

The undefined concept of the "public interest, convenience and necessity" provided room for new regulations and standards as the technology—and the broadcasting industry—changed. It also allowed Congress to prevent those it did not want heard on the airwaves from easily having a voice: socialists, labor groups and others.[290] In the signal reorganization that followed the Radio Act of 1927 and the Davis Amendment to that act, scores of small broadcasters lost their licenses or went out of business. The small broadcasters that survived, including various university radio stations, the Chicago Federation of Labor's radio station and the Paulist Fathers Catholic radio station in New York, found themselves in the midst of an uphill battle to preserve nonprofit broadcasting as Congress moved to pass the Communications Act of 1934.

Defining for-profit broadcasters and the networks as "general public service" stations and nonprofit broadcasters, labor unions, religious groups and schools as "propaganda" stations set the tone for legislation that came out quite clearly in favor of the commercial broadcasters.[291] The radio industry—at least the national networks—had worked hard to sell Congress and the general public on the concept that the "American system of broadcasting," which they had developed with commercially sponsored programs and the networks, was innately a United States system. As CBS president William Paley put it, "He who attacks the fundamentals of the American system attacks democracy itself."[292] Confirming the concerns of the nonprofit broadcasters, network-dominated, advertising-supported radio resulted in blocking the airing of unpopular or radical opinions and, under the guise of appealing to a mass audience, was woefully lacking in cultural, educational and public affairs programming.[293] Eleanor McClatchy's personal philosophy brought those programs to McClatchy Broadcasting listeners, but in an enterprise that had, by nature, to be commercial, her vision simply was not sustainable in the long run.

The system of broadcasting that developed in Sacramento and other Central Valley communities as part of the McClatchy Broadcasting Company became something of a hybrid. Beginning with a short broadcast schedule of local programming of interest to its listeners and engaging local talent, the McClatchy stations began selling advertising in the late 1920s. But even as their media holdings grew, network affiliations were put in place and a California-wide radio network was established, the McClatchy stations continued to focus on broadcasting programs that might appeal to the interests of their local audience. Had Carlos McClatchy not died in 1933, it is possible that what became the McClatchy Broadcasting Company would have developed along decidedly commercial lines and been more profitable in the long term.

Eleanor's goal was always to operate the business in a manner similar to what she felt her father would have wanted. But her adherence to C.K.'s philosophy of how a newspaper should run and the service a newspaper offered to the public were at odds with her vision of the public service function of radio broadcasting in a country that solidly placed itself on the side of commercial, for-profit broadcasting. Newspapers, including the *Sacramento Bee*, ran advertisements as a means of supporting the newsgathering, writing and publishing operation. Why should the broadcasting side of the business be any different?

This book is not, however, intended to be a history of radio in general. Using archival material, newspapers, government documents and business and radio industry periodicals of broadcasting's early decades, I have explored the business history of one West Coast company's early entry into and development of local and regional radio in California from the beginning of the 1920s into the 1980s. The McClatchy Company—and, by extension, the McClatchy family, who were the essence of the company from the late nineteenth through most of the twentieth centuries—illustrates how different radio development was for a regional business located far from the national networks, the industry lobbies and the point of legislative and governmental control. While many historians have looked at several angles of radio's development, from the technical and the regulatory to the cultural and debates over advertising and radio's financial business model, their work has been primarily focused on those regions of the United States where radio had its initial corporate launch, where the national networks developed and where legislation governing the new medium was debated, passed and amended.

This book takes a different approach. Our unique northern California broadcast radio story is told by looking at broadcast radio's early development away from the epicenters of broadcasting—the Northeast and Midwest—and away from the center of regulation, Washington, D.C., to see how national broadcast trends and the implementation of federal regulation affected broadcasting for low-powered radio stations serving regional audiences.

Examining Eleanor's use of radio in the public interest, what she would have called public service, gives some sense of what radio throughout the United States might have been if commercial, for-profit broadcasters and networks had not won the "debate" in the 1930s when the Communications Act of 1934 solidified the for-profit position as the "American system." With education as one of her priorities, as evidenced by the 1941 *La Escuela Espanola del Aire de KFBK*, Eleanor McClatchy put in place a system that from 1945 to 1973 broadcast education programs for in-school listening five days a week and included teachers' manuals sent out to the school districts in the listening area. Called *KFBK* (or KMJ, KOH, KBEE) *Goes to School*, the programs grew out of the radio schools for teachers that had been developed by McClatchy's first educational director, Frances Frater. The programs, in spite of offers of sponsorship, remained entirely free of advertising, as did all radio education programs produced by McClatchy Broadcasting.[294]

Eleanor's desire to build the broadcasting side of the business resulted in an increase in radio holdings that included not only KFBK, KMJ, KWG, KERN and KOH, the stations developed by Carlos McClatchy, but also KFBK-FM, KMJ-FM, KBEE-AM, KBEE-FM, television stations KMJ in Fresno and KOVR in Sacramento and four cable television systems. In 1977, the McClatchy pursuit of broadcast primacy in the Greater Sacramento region resulted in a $43 million antitrust suit brought by the owner of rival newspaper the *Sacramento Union*. The *Union*'s owner alleged the McClatchy companies sought a "news monopoly" in California's Central Valley. McClatchy filed a countersuit, and after two years of legal arguments, both suits were dropped.[295]

Erwin Potts, who in 1989 became the first non-McClatchy chief executive officer of the company, first came to the *Sacramento Bee* in 1975 as director of newspaper business operations. Upon his arrival, he found a company at which there were no real budgets, no five-year plans and no savings provisions for equipment expansion. Money was spent as it came in, and an eighty-year-old Eleanor still insisted on having the final approval of every move the company made.[296] In 1978, Eleanor passed control of the McClatchy operations over to Carlos's son C.K. She died two years later, in 1980. By 1986, the McClatchy Company had completely divested itself of all radio and television broadcast holdings, choosing instead to redirect the

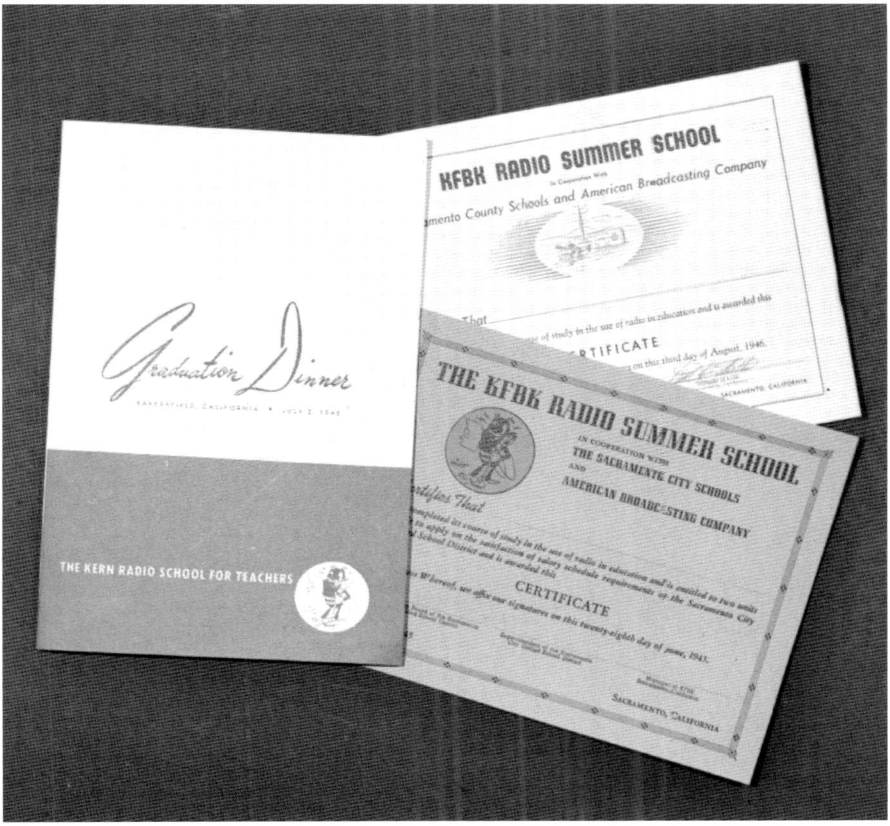

Eleanor's vision for broadcasting as a public service included education programs. *Center for Sacramento History*.

company back to a newspaper-only focus, and in 1988, McClatchy stock went on sale with a two-tier structure in place that allowed family control to be maintained. The purchase of the Knight Ridder newspaper chain in 2006 made McClatchy the country's second-largest newspaper chain in terms of circulation. Selling its *Minneapolis Star Tribune* newspaper to help pay the Knight Ridder debt dropped the McClatchy Company back to the third-largest U.S. newspaper chain. In 2014, the sale of the *Anchorage Daily News* set the company's holdings at twenty-nine daily newspapers in twenty-eight U.S. markets. Still a leading media company, today McClatchy focuses on print and digital.[297]

Although the McClatchys owned a number of radio stations in the 1920s and early 1930s that served the needs of the regional audience around

California governor Jerry Brown on KFBK toward the end of his second term as governor, circa 1981. KFBK was sold to Group W (Westinghouse) and today is part of iHeartRadio. *Center for Sacramento History.*

each station, they lacked influence in the debates over broadcast regulation. The McClatchys were successful in developing their broadcast holdings in spite of the multiple changes in broadcast regulation and enforcement in the early decades. They worked within their own definition of what constituted the public interest and based that definition on their understanding of serving the public—just as they did with the newspaper holdings. As broadcast pioneers, the McClatchys did not "make their own rules," but they did act swiftly and decisively to use radio to their best business advantage while, at the same time, understanding that without concern for the local constituency—the core definition of the public interest—their broadcast venture would not succeed. As Eleanor put it in notes for a broadcasting clinic:

> *Our papers and stations alike have been founded on the basic policies and principles of James McClatchy who believed in a free and democratic government, and the rights of the people. James' son C.K.*

> *promised his father that should* The Bee *ever lower its standards to allow the "ring of the cash register" to control its news or editorials, then should* The Bee *be sold and its name taken away. And I promised my father the same thing.*[298]

The vision—whether newspaper or radio—was always about the local audience.

NOTES

CHAPTER 1

1. Hiram Johnson to C.K. McClatchy, November 1, 1920, McClatchy Newspapers and Broadcasting Collection, Center for Sacramento History.
2. *Sacramento Bee*, "Newspaperman Foresaw Radio as Public Service Medium," October 1, 1948.
3. *Radio Broadcast*, "Who Will Ultimately do the Broadcasting?" April 1923, 522–26.
4. Paul Starr, *The Creation of the Media: Political Origins of Modern Communications* (2004; repr., New York: Basic books, 2005), 218–19.
5. Susan J. Douglas, *Inventing American Broadcasting: 1899–1922* (Baltimore: Johns Hopkins University Press, 1987), 216.
6. "Eighteen Years of Radio," *Congressional Digest* 7, no. 10 (October 1928), 255.
7. Starr, *Creation of the Media*, 218; "Eighteen Years of Radio," *Congressional Digest*, 255.
8. Starr, *Creation of the Media*, 219.
9. Daniel Czitrom, *Media and the American Mind: From Morse to McLuhan* (Chapel Hill: University of North Carolina Press, 1982), 68.
10. Erwin G. Krasnow, "The 'Public Interest' Standard: The Elusive Search for the Holy Grail," Briefing Paper Prepared for the Advisory Committee on Public Interest Obligations of Digital Television Broadcasters, October 22, 1997, http://www.govinfo.library.unt.edu/piac/octmtg/Krasnow.htm (accessed October 1, 2009), 3–4.

11. Douglas, *Inventing American Broadcasting*, 292–93.
12. Ibid., 297–99.
13. Ibid.
14. Czitrom, *Media and the American Mind*, 69.
15. Ibid.
16. Ibid., 70.
17. Ibid.
18. Ibid.; Starr, *Creation of the Media*, 327.
19. Douglas, *Inventing American Broadcasting*, 300–01.
20. Susan Smulyan, *Selling Radio: The Commercialization of American Broadcasting, 1920–1934* (Washington: Smithsonian Institution Press, 1994), 13–15.
21. Carl Dreher, "Is the Broadcast Listener at Fault?" *Radio Broadcast*, March 1924, 424–26; Czitrom, *Media and the American Mind*, 72–73.
22. Douglas, *Inventing American Broadcasting*, 309–10; J.M. McKibbin Jr., "The New Way to Make Americans," *Radio Broadcast*, January 1923, 238–39.
23. McKibbin, "New Way to Make Americans," 238–39.
24. Ibid.
25. Randall Patnode, "'What These People Need Is Radio:' New Technology, the Press, and Otherness in 1920s America," *Technology and Culture* 44, no. 2 (April 2003): 300.
26. "The Future of Radio," *New Republic* 40 (October 8, 1924): 136, quoted in Douglas, *Inventing American Broadcasting*, 313; Douglas, *Inventing American Broadcasting*, 315–16.
27. Julian Sivulka, *Soap, Sex, and Cigarettes: A Cultural History of American Advertising* (Belmont, CA: Wadsworth, 1998), 53, 142.
28. Derek Vaillant, "'Your Voice Came in Last Night…But I Thought it Sounded a Little Scared': Rural Radio Listening and 'Talking Back' During the Progressive Era in Wisconsin," in *Radio Reader: Essays in the Cultural History of Radio*, edited by Michele Hilmes and Jason Loviglio (New York: Routledge, 2002), 65.
29. Steven M. Avella, *Sacramento: Indomitable City* (Charleston, SC: Arcadia Publishing, 2003), 94.
30. Smulyan, *Selling Radio*, 12-15.
31. Sivulka, *Soap, Sex, and Cigarettes*, 183.
32. Douglas, *Inventing American Broadcasting*, 293.
33. Reginald A. Fessenden to S.M. Kintner, Westinghouse Electric, January 29, 1932, BANC MSS 72/115 z, Emil Jacob Simon and Lee De Forest collection, Bancroft Library, University of California–Berkeley; Douglas, *Inventing American Broadcasting*, 44–45.

34. Reginald A. Fessenden to S.M. Kintner, Westinghouse Electric, January 29, 1932, BANC MSS 72/115 z, Emil Jacob Simon and Lee De Forest collection, Bancroft Library, University of California–Berkeley.
35. Reminiscences of Sybil M. True, January 2, 1959, Columbia Oral History Archives, Rare Book & Manuscript Library, Columbia University in the City of New York, 9.
36. Ibid., 9–10.
37. Reminiscences of Joseph D. Cappa, March 21, 1959, Columbia Oral History Archives, Rare Book & Manuscript Library, Columbia University in the City of New York, 5.
38. Ibid., 17.

CHAPTER 2

39. Sivulka, *Soap, Sex, and Cigarettes*, 183; Stephen Fox, *The Mirror Makers: A History of American Advertising and Its Creators* (New York: William Morrow and Company, Inc., 1984), 152.
40. Fox, *Mirror Makers*, 152.
41. Sivulka, *Soap, Sex, and Cigarettes*, 183.
42. Clair L. Stout, Esquire, to John J. Hamlyn, November 9, 1948, McClatchy Newspapers and Broadcasting Collection, Center for Sacramento History.
43. License for Land Radio Station issued to the *Sacramento Bee* (James McClatchy Company) for station KVQ located at Seventh and I Streets in Sacramento, October 18, 1922, McClatchy Newspapers and Broadcasting Collection, Center for Sacramento History.
44. *Sacramento Bee*, "Hobrecht and the *Bee* Had First Radio Station in City," September 12, 1927; J.C. Hobrecht, "Pioneer Radio Man Recalls Early Days of Industry," *Sacramento Bee*, December 8, 1928.
45. *Sacramento Bee*, "Local Electroliers Designed by Hobrecht," September 12, 1927.
46. Ibid., "Success of Bee Radio Service Is Immediate," February 3, 1922; ibid., "Roseville Gets Thrill from Banjo Music," February 3, 1922; ibid., "Here Are Directions for Making Wireless Set," February 4, 1922.
47. Ibid., "Radio Plays a Prominent Part at State Fair," September 9, 1922; ibid., "Bee Radio Is Heard in Canada, 1,300 Miles Away," September 2, 1922; ibid., "1908–1932: A Champion of Causes," February 4, 2007.
48. Everett Davies, "Radio Station KFBK: A Brief History of Radio Broadcasting in Sacramento," undated manuscript, McClatchy

Newspapers and Broadcasting Collection, Center for Sacramento History; C.K. McClatchy to Hiram Johnson, September 20, 1928, McClatchy Newspapers and Broadcasting Collection, Center for Sacramento History.

49. *Sacramento Bee*, "1908–1932: A Champion of Causes"; and Bradley Riter, circa 1952, McClatchy Newspapers and Broadcasting Collection, Center for Sacramento History.

50. David Nasaw, *The Chief: The Life of William Randolph Hearst* (2000; repr., Boston: Mariner Books/Houghton Mifflin Company, 2001), 390–91.

51. *Radio Broadcast*, "Who Will Ultimately Do the Broadcasting?" April 1923, 522–26.

52. Winfield Barton, "What Broadcasting Does for a Newspaper," *Radio Broadcast*, February 1924, 344–46.

53. Ibid.

54. Michele Hilmes, *Radio Voices: American Broadcasting, 1922–1952* (Minneapolis: University of Minnesota Press, 1997), 69.

55. Agreement, James McClatchy Co. and Kimball-Upson Co., September 1, 1925, McClatchy Newspapers and Broadcasting Collection, Center for Sacramento History.

56. Memo to Fred Moore re: McClatchy Broadcasting Company history for Columbia University Managing Editors' Seminar, undated file copy, McClatchy Newspapers and Broadcasting Collection, Center for Sacramento History; *Sacramento Bee*, "1908–1932: A Champion of Causes."

57. Clifford John Doerksen, *American Babel: Rogue Radio Broadcasters of the Jazz Age* (Philadelphia: University of Pennsylvania Press, 2005), 9.

58. Ibid., 13, 17.

59. Michele Hilmes, *Hollywood and Broadcasting: From Radio to Cable* (Urbana: University of Illinois Press, 1990), 21–22.

60. Barton, "What Broadcasting Does for a Newspaper," 344.

61. Omara & Ormsbee, Inc., to W.H. James, September 15, 1925, McClatchy Newspapers and Broadcasting Collection, Center for Sacramento History.

62. W.H. James to Carlos McClatchy, September 17, 1925, McClatchy Newspapers and Broadcasting Collection, Center for Sacramento History.

63. L.A. Tripp to W.H. James, April 17, 1926, McClatchy Newspapers and Broadcasting Collection, Center for Sacramento History.

64. E.S. Riggins to W.H. James, January 15, 1929, McClatchy Newspapers and Broadcasting Collection, Center for Sacramento History.

65. R.K. Clark to W.H. James, January 7, 1928, McClatchy Newspapers and Broadcasting Collection, Center for Sacramento History.

66. Memo to Mr. James and Mr. Langdon re: KWG, Stockton, circa 1928, McClatchy Newspapers and Broadcasting Collection, Center for Sacramento History; Grover A. Whalen, "Radio Control," *Nation* 119, no. 3,081 (July 23, 1924), 90.

CHAPTER 3

67. *Sacramento Bee*, "Local Broadcaster Is Heard Throughout United States," December 8, 1928.
68. "Eighteen Years of Radio," *Congressional Digest*, 257.
69. Hiram W. Johnson to V.S. McClatchy, May 6, 1926, Hiram Johnson papers part III, BANC MSS C-B 581, Bancroft Library, University of California–Berkeley; Radio Act of 1927, Public Law No. 632, 69th Cong., 2nd sess., February 23, 1927.
70. Mark Goodman, "The Radio Act of 1927 as a Product of Progressivism," Media History Monographs 2, no. 2 (1998–99), http://www.scripps.ohiou.edu/mediahistory/mhmjour2-2.htm (accessed August 14, 2008); "Are Large Broadcasting Stations Violating the Radio Law?" *Congressional Digest* 7, no. 10 (October 1928), 271; David A. Moss and Michael R. Fein, "Radio Regulation Revisited: Coase, the FCC and the Public Interest," *Journal of Public History* 15, no. 4 (2003): 401.
71. "Eighteen Years of Radio," *Congressional Digest*, 257–258; Radio Act of 1927; "Radio Zones Established by Act of 1927," *Congressional Digest* 7, no. 10 (October 1928), 261.
72. Lizabeth Cohen, *Making a New Deal: Industrial Workers in Chicago, 1919–1939* (1990; repr., Cambridge: Cambridge University Press, 2009), 140–41.
73. Kimball-Upson Company to the Federal Radio Commission, July 23, 1927, McClatchy Newspapers and Broadcasting Collection, Center for Sacramento History.
74. Harold Lafount, FRC, to Kimball-Upson Co., February 18, 1928, McClatchy Newspapers and Broadcasting Collection, Center for Sacramento History.
75. W.H. James to C.B. Dodds, February 24, 1928, McClatchy Newspapers and Broadcasting Collection, Center for Sacramento History.
76. "The Davis Amendment to the Radio Act," *Congressional Digest* 7, no. 10 (October 1928), 261; "Will the Davis Amendment Bring Better Radio?" *Congressional Digest* 7, no. 10 (October 1928), 268; *New York Times*, "Radio Politics," March 14, 1928.

77. "Davis Amendment to the Radio Act," *Congressional Digest*, 261; "Problems Raised by the Davis Amendment," *Congressional Digest* 7, no. 10 (October 1928), 262.
78. Carlos McClatchy to W.H. James, circa 1928, McClatchy Newspapers and Broadcasting Collection, Center for Sacramento History.
79. *Sacramento Bee*, "Newspaperman Foresaw Radio as Public Service Medium," October 1, 1948.
80. Ralph K. Clark, "Advance in Radio is Remarkable," *Sacramento Bee*, December 8, 1928; Federal Radio Commission, Broadcasting Stations in the Fifth Zone, November 10, 1928, McClatchy Newspapers and Broadcasting Collection, Center for Sacramento History.
81. A.I. Maginnis to W.H. James, November 9, 1928, McClatchy Newspapers and Broadcasting Collection, Center for Sacramento History.
82. McClatchy Company timeline, circa 1965, McClatchy Newspapers and Broadcasting Collection, Center for Sacramento History.
83. Letters and telegrams between G.C. Hamilton of the *Sacramento Bee* and M. Connor in the office of Senator Hiram Johnson, November, 1929, McClatchy Newspapers and Broadcasting Collection, Center for Sacramento History.
84. G.C. Hamilton to Leigh Danenberg, *Bridgeport Herald*, March 17, 1931, McClatchy Newspapers and Broadcasting Collection, Center for Sacramento History.
85. *Sacramento Bee*, "Bee Station to Join Columbia Radio Hook-Up," January 15, 1930.
86. G.C. Hamilton to J.E. Hurley of Broadcast Advertising, Inc., September 18, 1930, McClatchy Newspapers and Broadcasting Collection, Center for Sacramento History.

CHAPTER 4

87. Elmo Griffith to KFBK, May 12, 1930, McClatchy Collection.
88. Vaillant, "Your Voice Came in Last Night," 68–69.
89. Dora Hoernlein to KFBK, March 3, 1930, McClatchy Newspapers and Broadcasting Collection, Center for Sacramento History.
90. "Report to Mr. William Randolph Hearst on Radio and Its Relation to His Newspapers," September 24, 1930, William Randolph Hearst papers, BANC MSS 77/121 c, carton 36, Bancroft Library, University of California–Berkeley.
91. U.S. census, 1930.

92. C.K. McClatchy to Hiram Johnson, December 22, 1930, McClatchy Newspapers and Broadcasting Collection, Center for Sacramento History.
93. G.C. Hamilton to M.A. Hollingshead, Campbell-Ewald Company, December 27, 1930, McClatchy Newspapers and Broadcasting Collection, Center for Sacramento History.
94. Bruce Lenthall, *Radio's America: The Great Depression and the Rise of Modern Mass Culture* (Chicago: University of Chicago Press, 2007), 67; Cohen, *Making a New Deal*, 214–18, 330–33.
95. Lenthall, *Radio's America*, 54–55.
96. Krasnow, "'Public Interest' Standard," 5.
97. Lucy A. Bishop, International Bible Students Association, to Manager, Bee Radio Station, January 26, 1931; G.C. Hamilton to Lucy A. Bishop, January 28, 1931, McClatchy Newspapers and Broadcasting Collection, Center for Sacramento History
98. "Report to Mr. William Randolph Hearst."
99. Michele Hilmes, "NBC and the Network Idea: Defining the 'American System,'" in *NBC: America's Network*, edited by Michele Hilmes (Berkeley: University of California Press, 2007), 16.
100. G.C. Hamilton, *Sacramento Bee*, to Leigh Danenberg, *Bridgeport Herald*, March 17, 1931, McClatchy Newspapers and Broadcasting Collection, Center for Sacramento History.
101. G.C. Hamilton, *Sacramento Bee*, to Leigh Danenberg, *Bridgeport Herald*, March 17, 1931, McClatchy Newspapers and Broadcasting Collection, Center for Sacramento History.
102. William Randolph Hearst to Emile J. Gough, director of Hearst Radio Service, October 22, 1930, William Randolph Hearst papers. BANC MSS 77/121 c, Bancroft Library, University of California–Berkeley.
103. Federal Communications Commission, *Report on Chain Broadcasting*, Commission Order No. 37, Docket No. 5060, May 1941, 3.
104. Ibid., 105–06.
105. Ibid.
106. *New York Times*, "New Radio Chain to Open April 5," March 26, 1927; ibid., "New Radio Chain Will Open Tonight," April 5, 1927.
107. Michael J. Socolow, "'Always in Friendly Competition': NBC and CBS in the First Decade of National Broadcasting," in *NBC: America's Network*, 31.
108. *Sacramento Bee*, "Today's Radio Events," August 1931.
109. Michele Hilmes, "Introduction to Part One: Broadcasting Begins, 1919–38," in *NBC: America's Network*, 3; ibid., "NBC and the Network Idea," 7; *New York Times*, "Says Radio Chain Is Losing Money," December 2, 1927.

Chapter 5

110. Carlos McClatchy to Grace Briggs, October 24, 1918, James and Susan McClatchy Collection Inventory, Center for Sacramento History.
111. *Sacramento Bee*, "1908–1932: A Champion of Causes."
112. Ibid.
113. Annette Kassis, *Weinstock's: Sacramento's Finest Department Store* (Charleston, SC: The History Press, 2012), 66–67.
114. *Sacramento Bee*, "1908–1932: A Champion of Causes"; ibid., "Weinstock-Lubin Offers to Conduct the Bee," December 13, 1920; Kassis, *Weinstock's: Sacramento's Finest Department Store*, 67.
115. Phebe Briggs McClatchy Conley, interviewed by Bob Molander, March 22, 1984, Fresno, California, James and Susan McClatchy Collection Inventory, Center for Sacramento History.
116. Ibid., interviewed by James McClatchy, January 1989, James and Susan McClatchy Collection Inventory, Center for Sacramento History.
117. Unpublished, undated recollections of Phebe Briggs McClatchy Conley, James and Susan McClatchy Collection Inventory, Center for Sacramento History.
118. Ibid.
119. Ibid.; Carlos McClatchy to Ella McClatchy, Western Union Telegram, January 4, 1918, James and Susan McClatchy Collection Inventory, Center for Sacramento History.
120. Unpublished, undated recollections of Phebe Briggs McClatchy Conley.
121. Conley, interviewed by Bob Molander; Carlos McClatchy to Mrs. William Briggs, October 24, 1918, James and Susan McClatchy Collection Inventory, Center for Sacramento History.
122. Carlos McClatchy to Mrs. William Briggs, October 24, 1918.
123. Ibid.
124. Unpublished, undated recollections of Phebe Briggs McClatchy Conley.
125. Ibid.
126. *Sacramento Bee*, "1908–1932: A Champion of Causes"; ibid., "C.K.'s Son Helped Expand Empire but Undercut Himself," February 4, 2007.
127. Ibid., "C.K.'s Son Helped Expand Empire but Undercut Himself," February 4, 2007.
128. Ibid.
129. Steve Wiegand, *Papers of Permanence: The First 150 Years of the McClatchy Company* (Sacramento: McClatchy Company, 2007), 140–41.
130. Conley, interviewed by Bob Molander.

131. Ibid.; Phebe Briggs McClatchy Conley interviewed by James McClatchy, December 26, 1984, James and Susan McClatchy Collection Inventory, Center for Sacramento History.
132. *Sacramento Bee*, "C.K.'s Son Helped Expand Empire but Undercut Himself."
133. Ibid.
134. Conley, interviewed by Bob Molander.
135. Ibid.
136. Phebe Briggs McClatchy Conley, interviewed by James McClatchy, March 1989, James and Susan McClatchy Collection Inventory, Center for Sacramento History.
137. C.K. McClatchy to Hiram Johnson, July 27, 1932, McClatchy Newspapers and Broadcasting Collection, Center for Sacramento History.
138. Ibid.
139. Ibid., July 30, 1932, McClatchy Newspapers and Broadcasting Collection, Center for Sacramento History.
140. Ibid., August 2, 1932, McClatchy Newspapers and Broadcasting Collection, Center for Sacramento History.
141. Ibid., August 12, 1932, McClatchy Newspapers and Broadcasting Collection, Center for Sacramento History.
142. *Sacramento Bee*, "Carlos K. McClatchy Dies of Pneumonia in San Mateo," January 17, 1933; Wiegand, *Papers of Permanence*, 163.
143. *Sacramento Bee*, "Carlos K. McClatchy Dies of Pneumonia in San Mateo."
144. Ibid., "C.K.'s Son Helped Expand Empire but Undercut Himself."
145. Nasaw, *Chief*, 358–59.

CHAPTER 6

146. C.K. McClatchy to Hiram Johnson, August 12, 1932.
147. *Sacramento Bee*, "C.K.'s Son Helped Expand Empire but Undercut Himself."
148. Voting Trust agreement between Charles K. McClatchy and Ella McClatchy, parties of the first part, and Ella K. McClatchy, Eleanor McClatchy, G.C. Hamilton and J. Earl Langdon, parties of the second part, February 27, 1933, McClatchy Newspapers and Broadcasting Collection, Center for Sacramento History.
149. C.K. McClatchy to the Trustees, February 21, 1936, McClatchy Newspapers and Broadcasting Collection, Center for Sacramento History.

150. Ibid.
151. Ibid.
152. Hilmes, "NBC and the Network Idea," 15–16.
153. Ibid.
154. Robert W. McChesney, "The Debate Over Public Policy and the Emergence of Commercial Broadcasting in the United States, 1927–1935," *Business and Economic History* 21 (1992): 174.
155. Hilmes, "NBC and the Network Idea," 15–16; McChesney, "Debate Over Public Policy," 173.
156. William S. Paley, November 29, 1937 address to the Second National Conference on Educational Broadcasting (Chicago, 1937).
157. McChesney, "Debate Over Public Policy," 173.
158. Ibid., 177; William S. Paley, November 29, 1937 address; Smulyan, *Selling Radio*, 139.
159. McChesney, "Debate Over Public Policy," 177.
160. Ibid., 178.
161. Ibid.
162. Ibid., 177–79; Smulyan, *Selling Radio*, 126; Starr, *Creation of the Media*, 360.
163. KPMG LLP Economic Consulting Services, "History of the Broadcast License Application Process," Prepared for the FCC as a Deliverable for the Study of "Estimation of Utilization Rates/Probabilities of Obtaining Broadcast Licenses from the FCC" (November 2000), http://www.fcc.gov/opportunity/meb_study/broadcast_lic_study_pt1.pdf (accessed February 17, 2010), 4.
164. James C. Young, "Is the Radio Newspaper Next?," *Radio Broadcast*, September, 1925, 575–76.
165. G.C. Hamilton, James McClatchy Company to Rogan Jones, West Coast Broadcasting Company, November 2, 1929, McClatchy Newspapers and Broadcasting Collection, Center for Sacramento History.
166. Gwenyth Jackaway, "The Press Radio War, 1924–1937: A Battle to Defend the Professional, Institutional, and Political Power of the Press" (PhD diss., University of Pennsylvania, 1992), 3–4.
167. E.H. Harris, "Radio and the Press," *Annals of the American Academy of Political and Social Science* 177 (January 1935); Clarence C. Dill, "Radio and the Press: A Contrary View," *Annals of the American Academy of Political and Social Science* 177 (January 1935).
168. *Sacramento Bee*, "The Sacramento Bee Kimball-Upson Radio Station Schedule," December 1928; ibid., "The Bee Radio Station Schedule," October 1930.

169. Mitchell V. Charnley, *News by Radio* (New York: MacMillan Company, 1948), 8.
170. Giraud Chester, "The Press-Radio War: 1933–1935," *Public Opinion Quarterly* 13, no. 2 (1949): 253–54.
171. Jackaway, "Press Radio War, 1924–1937," 94.
172. *Sacramento Bee*, "Tonight's Radio Events"; ibid., "Sacramento Night on KFRC," advertisement, December 1, 1928.
173. Charnley, *News by Radio*, 8–9.
174. Ibid.
175. Ibid., 13–15; Hilmes, *Only Connect*, 94.
176. Charnley, *News by Radio*, 12; Michele Hilmes, *Only Connect: A Cultural History of Broadcasting in the United States* (Belmont, CA: Wadsworth Group, 2002), 94.
177. Chester, "Press-Radio War," 254–56; Jackaway, "Press Radio War, 1924–1937," 137.
178. Chester, "Press-Radio War," 254–56; Jackaway, "Press Radio War, 1924–1937," 140.
179. *Sacramento Bee*, radio schedule, December 23, 1933.
180. Jackaway, "Press Radio War, 1924–1937," 142–46.
181. Chester, "Press-Radio War," 256; Hilmes, *Only Connect*, 94–95.
182. Chester, "Press-Radio War," 256–58; Jackaway, "Press Radio War, 1924–1937," 147.
183. Chester, "Press-Radio War," 257–59.
184. *Sacramento Bee*, "Listenin' in on the Bee Radio," April 1935 and November 1936.
185. Chester, "Press-Radio War," 263–64; Jackaway, "Press Radio War, 1924–1937," 158.
186. Bradley Riter, circa 1952, McClatchy Newspapers and Broadcasting Collection, Series V, Box 25, 2005/054/0831, Center for Sacramento History.
187. Ibid.; "History of Radio Station KFBK," circa 1975, McClatchy Newspapers and Broadcasting Collection, Center for Sacramento History.
188. *Sacramento Bee*, "1933–1957: Hard Times, Boom Times," February 4, 2007.
189. Federal Communications Commission, *Report on Chain Broadcasting*, 103.
190. Ibid.; Bradley Riter, notes on company history, circa 1951, McClatchy Newspapers and Broadcasting Collection, Center for Sacramento History.
191. *Sacramento Bee*, "Six Key Stations Comprise Radio Network in State," December 2, 1936.
192. Nasaw, *Chief*, 527–42.

193. Federal Communications Commission, *Report on Chain Broadcasting*, 308–09; *Sacramento Bee*, "McClatchy Radio Assumes Control of State System," November 6, 1937.
194. *Sacramento Bee*, "McClatchy Radio Assumes Control of State System," November 6, 1937.
195. Federal Communications Commission, *Report on Chain Broadcasting*, 103; Riter, notes on company history, circa 1951, McClatchy Collection.
196. *Sacramento Bee*, "McClatchy Radio Assumes Control of State System."

CHAPTER 7

197. Conley, interviewed by James McClatchy, March 1989.
198. Ibid.; Wiegand, *Papers of Permanence*, 176.
199. C.K. McClatchy to Eleanor McClatchy, February 22, 1936, McClatchy Newspapers and Broadcasting Collection, Center for Sacramento History.
200. *Sacramento Bee*, "1933–1957: Hard Times, Boom Times."
201. "The McClatchy Broadcasting Company Presents: Facsimile, the Newspaper of the Air," brochure for the 1939 Convention of the Pacific Coast Division of the American Association of Advertising Agencies (AAAA), October 26, 1939, McClatchy Newspapers and Broadcasting Collection, Center for Sacramento History; *Sacramento Bee*, "McClatchy Radio Newspaper of Air Is Approved," November 9, 1937.
202. *Business Week*, "Network Daily Paper: Californians Receive Morning Facsimile Broadcast from Two Stations," February 25, 1939, 35–36; "McClatchy Broadcasting Company Presents: Facsimile, the Newspaper of the Air."
203. *Sacramento Bee*, "1933–1957: Hard Times, Boom Times."
204. *Business Week*, "Network Daily Paper," 36.
205. *Sacramento Bee*, "1933–1957: Hard Times, Boom Times"; *Business Week*, "Network Daily Paper," 35; *Sacramento Bee*, "McClatchy Radio Newspaper of Air Is Approved."
206. Theodore C. Streibert and Fulton Lewis Jr., "Radio as a News Medium," *Annals of the American Academy of Political and Social Science* 213 (January 1941): 61.
207. "McClatchy Broadcasting Company Presents Facsimile: The Newspaper of the Air."
208. *Sacramento Bee*, "1933–1957: Hard Times, Boom Times."

209. Riter, circa 1952, McClatchy Collection; Dan McGrath, "Business Move Signals End of a Radio Station Yet Again," *Sacramento Bee*, November 2, 1994; Walt Wiley, "The Rise and Fall of KROY's Beacon-Turned-Blemish Tower," *Sacramento Bee*, June 24, 2005.
210. Riter, circa 1952, McClatchy Collection; *Sacramento Bee*, "1908–1932: A Champion of Causes"; Wiegand, *Papers of Permanence*, 154.
211. "The Pro & Con Monthly," *Congressional Digest* 17, no. 12 (December 1938).
212. Christopher H. Sterling, "Breaking Chains: NBC and the FCC Network Inquiry, 1938–1943," in *NBC: America's Network*, 85–86.
213. Jim Cox, *American Radio Networks: A History* (Jefferson, NC: McFarland & Company, Inc., 2009), 72.
214. Ibid., 74–75; Socolow, "Always in Friendly Competition," 36.
215. Socolow, "Always in Friendly Competition," 36.
216. Sterling, "Breaking Chains," 86.
217. Hilmes, *Only Connect*, 70–71.
218. "Principles and Practices of Network Radio Broadcasting: Testimony of David Sarnoff," before the Federal Communications Commission, Washington, D.C., November 14, 1938, and May 17, 1939, 12.
219. Ibid., 21–22.
220. Federal Communications Commission, *Report on Chain Broadcasting*, 4.
221. Ibid., 88.
222. Ibid., 88–89.
223. Ibid., 44–45.
224. Ibid., 66.
225. Ibid., 91–92; Herbert H. Rosenberg, "Program Content—A Criterion of Public Interest in FCC Licensing," *Western Political Quarterly* 2, no. 3 (September 1949): 382.
226. Draft of a letter to the Blue Network Company, Inc., circa 1941, McClatchy Newspapers and Broadcasting Collection, Center for Sacramento History.
227. Rosenberg, "Program Content—A Criterion of Public Interest in FCC Licensing," 382.
228. Fred Weber, "Mutual's White Paper: Analyzing the Causes and Effects of 1. The Federal Communications Commission Report on Chain Broadcasting, and 2. The Mutual-ASCAP Agreement," May 23, 1941, 2.
229. Ibid., 4.
230. Ibid., "Mutual's Second White Paper: Analyzing the Federal Communications Commission's Recent Revision of Its Chain Broadcasting Regulations," October 20, 1941, 17.

231. Hilmes, "NBC and the Network Idea," 22; Sterling, "Breaking Chains," 90–95; KPMG LLP Economic Consulting Services, "History of the Broadcast License Application Process," 18.
232. Wiegand, *Papers of Permanence*, 182–83.
233. Michael J. Socolow, "'News is a Weapon': Domestic Radio Propaganda and Broadcast Journalism in America, 1936–1944," *American Journalism* 24, no. 3 (Summer 2007): 121.
234. McClatchy Broadcasting Company, "General Procedures and Rules to Follow in Preparing and Announcing Newscasts," circa 1937–40, McClatchy Newspapers and Broadcasting Collection, Center for Sacramento History.
235. Ibid.
236. *Sacramento Bee*, "As Smooth as an Old Gold" advertisement, March 9, 1933.
237. Ibid.
238. G.C. Hamilton to J.E. Hurley, Broadcast Advertising, Inc., September 18, 1930, McClatchy Newspapers and Broadcasting Collection, Center for Sacramento History.
239. Helen Woodward, "A Cigarette by Any Name…," *Nation*, August 13, 1938, 151–54.
240. Fox, *Mirror Makers*, 154–57.
241. Ibid., 118; Sivulka, *Soap, Sex, and Cigarettes*, 219.
242. *Business Week*, "Neither Sponsors Nor Stations Heed Radio Listeners' Grumbling," February 10, 1932, 18–19.
243. Kate Lacey, "Radio in the Great Depression: Promotional Culture, Public Service, and Propaganda," in *Radio Reader*, 23; Meg Jacobs, *Pocketbook Politics: Economic Citizenship in Twentieth-Century America* (2005; repr., Princeton, NJ: Princeton University Press, 2007), 96–135.
244. *Sacramento Bee*, "Listenin' in on the Bee Radio," November 25, 1936; ibid., "On the Air Today," November 8, 1937.
245. Ibid., "More Auto Radios are Predicted for Industry," November 25, 1936.
246. Riter, circa 1952, McClatchy Collection.
247. *Sacramento Bee*, "Two Busy Bees, Straight from the Pen of Walt Disney, Make Appearance," September 4, 1943.
248. Wiegand, *Papers of Permanence*, 188–89.
249. *Sacramento Bee*, "On the Bee Radio," December 2, 1942; ibid., "Navy Mother Is to Give Report Tonight," November 1942.
250. Station file notes for "The Story of KFBK," circa 1950, McClatchy Newspapers and Broadcasting Collection, Center for Sacramento History.

CHAPTER 8

251. Charles Hull Wolfe, *Modern Radio Advertising* (New York: Funk & Wagnalls Company, 1949), 47.
252. Ibid., 48.
253. Ibid., 51–54.
254. C.H. Sandage, *Radio Advertising for Retailers* (Cambridge, MA: Harvard University Press, 1948), 9–10.
255. *Business Week*, "Spot Radio Prospers," June 27, 1936, 29–30.
256. "Analysis of Station Broadcast Revenues, Preliminary Report" for Federal Communications Commission, December 31, 1945, McClatchy Newspapers and Broadcasting Collection, Center for Sacramento History. Figures listed in the preliminary report are unaudited.
257. Lizabeth Cohen, *A Consumers' Republic: The Politics of Mass Consumption in Postwar America* (2003; repr., New York: Vintage Books, 2004), 112–19.
258. Industrial Survey Associates, San Francisco, "The Economy of the Sacramento Area…and Its Potentials for Industrial Development: A Report Prepared for the Sacramento County Chamber of Commerce," June 1951, McClatchy Newspapers and Broadcasting Collection, Center for Sacramento History.
259. Ibid., quoting V.B. Stanbery in an article for *Frontier*.
260. Kassis, *Weinstock's: Sacramento's Finest Department Store*, 90; Avella, *Sacramento: Indomitable City*, 116–18; *Sacramento Facts 1953: The Land the Lord Remembered* (Sacramento, CA: Sacramento Chamber of Commerce, 1953), 7–11.
261. Steven M. Avella, *The Good Life: Sacramento's Consumer Culture* (Charleston, SC: Arcadia Publishing, 2008), 135–37.
262. Enid Day, *Radio Broadcasting for Retailers* (New York: Fairchild Publishing Co., 1947), 3.
263. Kassis, *Weinstock's: Sacramento's Finest Department Store*, 100; *Sacramento Bee*, "Weinstock-Lubin Wins Window Display Awards," March 13, 1952; *Sacramento Bee*, "Weinstock-Lubin Wins Award for Ad in Bee," January 4, 1955; *Sacramento Bee*, "KFBK AM and FM Tune in Time," September 2, 1953.
264. Cohen, *Consumers' Republic*, 123.
265. Ibid., 124–29.
266. Avella, *Good Life*, 18-19.
267. Cohen, *Consumers' Republic*, 123–24.
268. *Sacramento Bee*, Maleville Bros. advertisement, October 1, 1948, Dave Henry Collection, Center for Sacramento History.

269. Ibid., "Times to Remember" and "KFBK Will Originate Web Program Here Next Week," October 1, 1948, Dave Henry Collection, Center for Sacramento History.
270. Ibid., "Station Has Well Rounded Farm Schedule," October 1, 1948, Dave Henry Collection, Center for Sacramento History.
271. Wiegand, *Papers of Permanence*, 182–83.
272. Station file notes for "The Story of KFBK," circa 1950, McClatchy Collection; Wiegand, *Papers of Permanence*, 182–83.
273. Station file notes for "The Story of KFBK," circa 1950, McClatchy Collection.
274. Wiegand, *Papers of Permanence*, 182–83.
275. Bob Foreman, "What's Happening in Radio?" *Advertising & Selling and the Advertising Agency*, February 1949, 31.
276. "She Gave Up Desired Career to Fulfill Her Family Duty" in *Sacramento Bee*, "1933–1957: Hard Times, Boom Times"; Riter, circa 1952, McClatchy Collection.
277. "She Gave Up Desired Career to Fulfill Her Family Duty" in *Sacramento Bee*, "1933–1957: Hard Times, Boom Times"; Wiegand, *Papers of Permanence*, 194.
278. James McClatchy to Eleanor McClatchy, August 14, 1956, James and Susan McClatchy Collection Inventory, Center for Sacramento History.
279. Ibid.
280. G.C. Hamilton to Leigh Canenberg, *Bridgeport Herald*, March 17, 1931, McClatchy Collection.
281. Sacramento-area agricultural business dated in Industrial Survey Associates, "Economy of the Sacramento Area," McClatchy Collection.
282. Wiegand, *Papers of Permanence*, 206–07.
283. Ibid.
284. Ibid.
285. Script for inaugural KOVR broadcast, April 1, 1965, McClatchy Newspapers and Broadcasting Collection, Center for Sacramento History.

Chapter 9

286. "Potter Stewart," Oyez: U.S. Supreme Court Media, http://www.oyez.org/justices/potter_stewart/ (accessed April 11, 2010).
287. Krasnow, "'Public Interest' Standard," 4.
288. Ibid.

289. "Eighteen Years of Radio" and "What the Radio Act of 1927 Provides," *Congressional Digest* 7, no. 10 (October 1928), 255–58; *New York Times*, "New Radio Bill Introduced; Hearings Fixed for January," December 20, 1925.
290. Goodman, "Radio Act of 1927," 9.
291. Hilmes, "NBC and the Network Idea," 15–16.
292. McChesney, "Debate Over Public Policy," 177; Paley, November 29, 1937 address.
293. McChesney, "Debate Over Public Policy," 174–76.
294. "McClatchy: Long and Distinguished Service in the Public Interest," circa 1974, McClatchy Newspapers and Broadcasting Collection, Center for Sacramento History.
295. *Sacramento Bee*, "1933–1957: Hard Times, Boom Times"; ibid. "1958–1982: Sticking to the Status Quo," February 4, 2007.
296. Wiegand, *Papers of Permanence*, 237.
297. *Sacramento Bee*, "1933–1957: Hard Times, Boom Times"; ibid. "1958–1982: Sticking to the Status Quo"; "About Us," The McClatchy Company, http://www.mcclatchy.com/about_us/ (accessed January 25, 2015).
298. Eleanor McClatchy notes, broadcasting clinic, December 1, 1969, James and Susan McClatchy Collection Inventory, Center for Sacramento History.

INDEX

V

W

ABOUT THE AUTHOR

Annette Kassis is a writer living in the Sacramento area and author of the recent History Press titles *Prohibition in Sacramento: Moralizers & Bootleggers in the Wettest City in the Nation* and *Weinstock's: Sacramento's Finest Department Store*. Formerly co-owner of the Sacramento-based advertising agency K&H Marketing, LLC, Annette is currently the director of Consumer & Brand Marketing for the California Beef Council and serves on the board of the Sacramento History Alliance. She holds a master's degree in history from California State University–Sacramento.